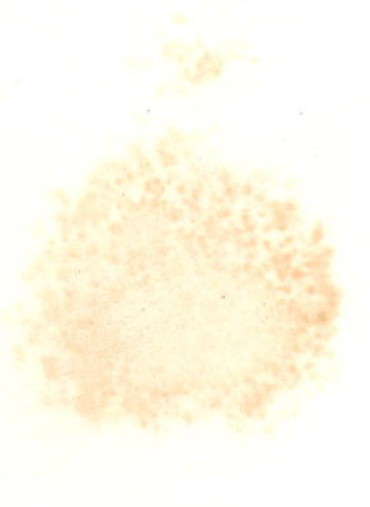

AF531548

About this Book

More than seven centuries ago an obscure Mongol nomad forged an empire from the Black Sea to the Pacific Ocean. His name was Temujin, later known as Genghis Khan, perhaps the greatest military genius the world has ever seen and certainly one of the most romanticized figures in history.

But historians, as Mr Ralph Fox says, have never given any satisfactory explanation for the great revolution in human progress that Genghis Khan produced. 'Some ascribed it to the genius of one man, but how such a man could rise from such obscurity they did not say. Some put it down to a sudden flowering of the Mongol national spirit, but why a great national spirit should suddenly appear in a people without a history, without a national existence, they did not tell us. Others again sought the truth in the supposed simplicity and freedom of nomad life proving its superiority over more decadent and cultured peoples.' And, obviously, the modern historian 'cannot be satisfied with such easy reasoning.' Mr Fox is therefore to be congratulated on painting a picture of Genghis Khan and his times that is as compelling as M. Leon Cahun's romantic *Introduction to the History of Asia* and as objective as Professor Vladimirtsov's *Chingis-Khan.* Widely travelled, a fine linguist, a painstaking and critical student, an effective writer, it is not surprising that he produced a fascinating biography that is also a rational contribution to the story of human development.

It would be easy to take an individualistic view of Genghis Khan but Mr Fox presents him as a function of his time, and his conquests as the logical development of the social life and history of his people, not as a series of inexplicable natural explosions 'terrifying and spontaneous like the awful thunderstorms of the late summer in the Gobi.' The rise of Genghis Khan coincided with the breaking up of the old clan system and the evident necessity for one lord to 'beat the others, to shatter the last fragments of the old patriarchal life and build a new one on the basis of the new relationships. Temujin-Chingis was born at a time of crisis among his own people when all was ready for the leader who should build the new society. It was his fate also to be born when the two great feudal states on either side of him, the Khwarizmian Empire in Central Asia and the Kin Empire in China, were in full decay. It was this combination which made it the destiny of the Mongol nomad to become the Emperor of the world, the greatest conqueror since Alexander the godlike, prince of Macedon.'

GENGHIS KHAN

GENGHIS KHAN

Ralph Winston Fox

First Published 1936
First LG Edition 2018

ISBN 978–93–83723–30–0

Published by
LG PUBLISHERS DISTRIBUTORS
49, Street No. 14, Pratap Nagar,
Mayur Vihar Phase I, Delhi 110091
Email: lgpdist@gmail.com

Printed at
Sapra Brothers, Delhi 110 092

Preface

The pitfalls which beset the writing of such a book as this are obvious, but by no means therefore easy to avoid. The very name of Genghis-Khan has such romantic associations that it is hard to prevent oneself being carried away by them into the writing of a mere picturesque tale. On the other hand, the fact that there is no book accessible to the general reader, or even to the historian, which fits him into his place in history, compels one to attempt the difficult task of combining popularity with some amount of accuracy, while avoiding either the dullness of pure scholarship or the vulgarizing that arises from a too superficial acquaintance with one's subject. How far all these dangers have been overcome must be left to the reader to decide, in consultation with the specialist.

At least if I have succeeded in giving a credible account of one of the most astonishing and neglected pages in the bloody past of our world, in showing that it may mean something to us to-day, face to face with massacres more appalling than any committed by Hun or Mongol cavalryman, then the labour which has gone to making the book will not be lost.

More than one modern intellectual, wearied by what seems to him the senseless slaughter of men and murder of human culture in our own day, has turned towards those grim and dark figures of the childhood of our age, Attila and Genghis-Khan, to find an expressive symbol for his pessimism. More than one admirer of militarism and lover of war has found in them also the justification for his own life selflessly devoted to depriving others of theirs.

I have nothing in common with either of these. I have sought to picture the man and his age as they were, confident that reality will always uncover its own secret motive springs and that life does not deny itself. That is the privilege of men whose own life has ceased to have meaning and not of humanity as a whole, in its historical development. In short, I fear that the lover of blood and the hater of his own kind may both be dissatisfied with the Genghis-Khan of history whom they will, I hope, find in this book.

Indeed, after the first pages, the very name of Genghis-Khan disappears and in his place appears the Mongol Temujin, who won for himself the imperial title of Chingis-Khan when he united his people into a nation. It is another difficulty, for the ordinary reader knows the name Genghis, but Chingis means nothing to him. Well, let him now put Genghis aside, for he is legend, and replace him by the historical reality of Temujin, the Chingis-Khan.

Save for Professor Vladimirtsov's brilliant essay, *The Life of Chingis Khan*, the English translation of which was published in 1930, this is the only book upon the subject in English based on a study of original sources. I am only too strongly aware, however, of my deficiencies in this regard. Save for a rudimentary knowledge of Turkish, I know no Eastern languages, and have been dependent entirely on translations. At least two important books, which are untranslated into European languages, have remained inaccessible to me except through summaries.

The defect, however, owing to the work of such great scholars in Central Asian history as Professor Paul Pelliot and the Russian academicians Barthold and Vladimirtsov, is not so fatal as once it might have been. Their work has so cleared the ground and so carefully analysed all the sources, that it is possible to avoid most of the pitfalls that beset the historians of the last century.

The chief sources which I have used are the Persian history of Rashid ed-Din, in the Russian translation of Berezine, and the Mongol *Secret History*, translated from the Chinese by the Russian monk Palladius. To these may be added the Chinese histories of Chingis, woven into one narrative by the late R. K. Douglas, the Arabic chronicle of Ibn el-Athir, the Persian history of Juzjani (Nasiri) and the memoirs of Mohammed En-Nesawi written in the form of the biography of his master, the Sultan Jelal ed-Din. This last I have found particularly valuable as the personal impressions of one who played an active part in the resistance to the Mongols. Mr Arthur Waley's edition of the travels of the Taoist monk Ch'ang Ch'un has also been invaluable.

The German translation of the Mongol history of Sanan Setsen is very unreliable and I have used it little. Lastly, the great collections of medieval travellers to China edited by Yule and Cordier, and their edition of *Marco Polo*, have been among the most important of the works I have used.

Of secondary sources by far the most valuable are the two books by Vladimirtsov, the greatest of modern Mongolists, Barthold's classic *Turkestan* and the old work of the Dutch historian D'Ohsson. I should like particularly to acknowledge my debt to the late Professor Vladimirtsov's *Social Structure of the Mongols.* This posthumous work only came into my hands when my own studies were finished. The conclusions I had formed corresponded almost exactly with those of Vladimirtsov, but his were founded on such wide and scholarly knowledge that they could not but give better form and securer authority to my own rough approximations.

Lastly, my sincere thanks are due to Sir E. Denison Ross, Director of the School of Oriental Studies, for the constant help and advice he has given me throughout.

EUROPE AND ASIA
about 1210
Before the Mongol Conquest
English Miles
0 100 200 400 600 800
Great Wall
Frontiers
GERMANY
HUNGARY
RUSSIAN
STATES
KIPCHAK
BLACK SEA
Constantinople
SELJUKS
MEDITERRANEAN SEA
SYRIA
ARMENIA
GEORGIA
TREBIZOND
Sea of Azov
Don
Volga
Ural
Sarai
Astrakhan
Turgai
Irtysh
Yenesei
CASPIAN SEA
Urganj
KHWARIZM
Kizil Kum Desert
KHWARIZMIAN EMPIRE
Otrar
Shash
Khojend
FERGHANA
Samarkand
SOGHDIANA
Balkh
Merv
Nishapur
KHORASAN
Herat
Hindu Kush
AFGHANISTAN
Kandahar
Ghazna
Peshawar
Lahore
PUNJAB
Indus
INDIA
Himalaya
PAMIR
Kashgar
Yarkand
Tarim
Lop Nor
TIBET
Baghdad
Tigris
Euphrates
IRAK
Ray
Ispahan
LURISTAN
PERSIA
(IRAN)
FARS
PERSIAN GULF
Ormuz
ARABIA
RED SEA
Tabriz
Maragha
Tiflis
KURDISTAN
Lake Balkash
Chu
Ili
Almalik
Ala-Tau
Balasagun
Bishbalig
Turfan
UIGHURS
KARA-KHITAI
SIBERIA
TURKS
KIRGHIZ
OIRAT
Lake Baikal
NAIMAN
Kara-Korum
MERKIT
KERAIT
MONGOLS
Onon
Karulan
TATARS
KONGIRAT
Amur
JURJENS
MONGOL
Gobi Desert
ONGUT
HSI-HSIA (TANGUT)
Kara-Khoto
Kanchu
Great Wall
Hwang-Ho
KIN EMPIRE
Peking
SHANTUNG
Grand Canal
KHITANS
KOREA
HONAN
Wei-Ho
Yang-Tse
Hangchow
SUNG EMPIRE
Canton
R.C.

CONTENTS

PART I

The Mongols and their World

1. Prelude of East and West

THIRTEEN years ago a young Englishman, shivering with cold inside his sheepskin coat, his face as yellow with malaria as the crumbling loess and frozen sand-drifts around him, stood by the single track of railway that runs through the delta of the Jaxartes by the Aral Sea, on its way to the deep valleys and fertile plains of the land of the Uzbek Turks. He was watching something moving along the track, and it was not a train. Trains also called for attention, since they were very rare and always brought news. But this time the cold serpent track that disappeared into the bare yellow hills, with their sharp, cardboard outlines, was interesting for the fact that a man was walking along it.

Men do not walk in this part of the world, they ride on horses or camels. If they are so poor they cannot do either they steal a ride on a train, or, rather, thirteen years ago they simply took a ride on a train, for no one tried to stop them. All the more remarkable then, was this horseless man stumbling along the ties, coming nearer till he reached the place where the young man was standing and who then, with bent head, never looking up, stumbled on past him.

That horseless man made an unforgettable impression. The thermometer was well below zero. He had no sheep-skin, the brown skin showed through the tatters of his rags. His square, Mongol face with its sparse hairs, was covered with frost-sores, his eyes were red with sun, with exposure, with disease. An ancient fur cap kept head and ears warm, but this was a man with nothing, neither horse, nor wife, nor tent, nothing but a bare spark of life that forced those short, arched legs from place to place in accordance with some deep instinct of his nomad consciousness. He could endure, but it would be too much to say he suffered. Yes, above all he could endure. In that bare and frozen steppe where nothing grew, whence the tents had disappeared in the autumn migrations and only a few mud huts remained by river and lake, he was able to live still, though he could neither see, nor feel, nor understand, only move.

The young man who watched him pass had spent the whole summer with the nomad Kirghiz-Kazaks, but nothing in their strange life had so impressed him as the sight of this one man. For thirteen years the figure of that man has gone stumbling throughh is consciousness till it has at last brought him to write this book. The man was a Kazak, of Turkish race, and this book is the story of the rise of the Mongol Empire. Turk and Mongol, however, were once of one race, and perhaps his own ignorance, perhaps some inherited traditional memory common to all Europeans, set his mind thinking of the empire of Temujin-Chingis, whom we call Genghis-Khan, rather than of the earlier nomad empire of the Turks, or of the great settled civilizations of Central Asia. After all, the first travellers from Europe who crossed those steppes, and he was standing on one of the greatest of the old trade routes when that man stumbled by, were on their way to the courts of the Great Khans of High Tartary, the sons and grandsons of Chingis.

Who was Chingis, how came he to conquer with his horsemen such a vast amount of the whole space of the world? The ordinary history books, even the works of specialists, give no real answer. It has remained a mystery, even to them. The Mongols, like the man on the line, had come from nowhere, stayed a moment and gone. The process was picturesquely and even grandly described. There can be few more romantic pieces of historical writing than the book of M Léon Cahun, for example. But no cause for this great revolution in human history that could satisfy the reader, was given. Some ascribed it to the genius of one man, but how such a man could arise from such obscurity, they did not say. Some put it down to a sudden flowering of the Mongol national spirit, but why a great national spirit should suddenly appear in a people without a history, without a national existence, they did not tell us. Others again sought the truth in the supposed simplicity and freedom of nomad life proving its superiority over more decadent and cultured peoples.

Yet the modern historian cannot be satisfied with such easy reasoning. Human history, the life of nations, the development of genius, is far more subtle and many-sided. It will fit into no such simple frames as these.

It is a problem that cries for solution. For the Mongols are again called on to play a decisive part in history. The one Asiatic country which the children of Chingis failed to conquer, Japan, is seeking to re-establish the Pan-Asiatic empire over which the Mongols once ruled. In that attempt the Mongol people must play a key part. Mr Owen Lattimore, who knows Mongolia as well as any man, is right when he warns us that: 'There is no telling when or how, or on what frontier, a tribal war may start in Mongolia. Still less can it be foreseen how far that war might spread. The powers of the world may plan for peace, but Manchukuo was fashioned under the star of war, and the star shines now towards Mongolia. Empires, in the end, are masters of the men who build them: you cannot claim a great destiny and then refuse to follow it up.'

The Mongols are once more involved in a great clash of classes and of nations in the East. They are forcing Europe to understand that the little people which once conquered the world is still alive, still conscious of itself, that it has passed the stage of dumb endurance, and is a nation once again, even though a very small one. Interest in their past is re-awakened and has a new significance. Inevitably it must centre around the great man who first brought them out of obscurity and made them a force in world history. Temujin-Chingis can no longer remain either a mystery or a legend.

No problem in world history is more obscure or more fascinating. A small and unknown people, whose first important appearance in history dates only from the middle of the twelfth century when they are recorded as taking part in the tribal warfare on the Chinese northern frontier, in some fifty years conquers almost the whole of Asia and sends raiding parties into Europe. The very name Mongol, the name of a legendary chief, is only adopted by them as a nation after Chingis, their great leader, has made them the founders of an empire.

A son is born to a nomad adventurer in the rugged country east of Lake Baikal. The father is poisoned by enemies while the son is still a boy, leaving him completely defenceless. Ignorant, illiterate, barely able to trap or slay sufficient to keep himself and his mother and brothers alive, a temptation to every strong enemy at a time when all men were his enemies, Temujin lives an obscure and hunted life until manhood. The flower of his years is full of defeat and the worst of humiliations, not until he is in middle age does he win for himself a secure position among the surrounding tribes, not till he is in his fiftieth year does he begin his astonishing career of conquest.

Yet when the time comes he shows himself to be the leader of an army unequalled in the world of that time for organization, discipline and the power of decisive and swift manœuvre. These ignorant nomads display an ability to make use of technique, to listen to wise counsel, that shames their enemies. Temujin-Chingis himself appears as one of the great military and political geniuses of all time, controlling and planning conquests that demand powers of organization, mastery of strategy, wise calculation and strength of will such as few men have ever possessed.

The movement in world history which his armies started was far-reaching in its effects. It may be that in the Mongol conquests we have one of the great turning points in history, that the fate of Europe and of Asia was here decided for many centuries to come. Viewed even superficially the effects were enormous. A Mongol dynasty was established over the whole of China, Mongols ruled in Central Asia, in Persia, over the Russian steppes, their princes and descendants crossed the great mountain barrier into India. They shook the whole of Eastern Europe. What people, so small in numbers and poor in resources, has ever done so much?

But violence, the action of armies, conquest and destruction, which appear to be the chief characteristics of the Mongol heritage, are not things in themselves. The believers in the mystical force of pure action have always been ready to bow before the image of Genghis-Khan as the embodiment of their belief. Those who hate war as such have on the other hand seen here only the pyramids of skulls and the stinking slime of decaying bodies described by the Persian historian Juzjani. War, however, is not history itself but only an instrument of history. Violent changes are only wrought in men's affairs when all the conditions for those changes are already ripe.

The sober-minded inquirer, in considering the story of the Mongols and their leader, cannot to-day rest content with the explanation which satisfied the thinkers of the Middle Ages, that here we have some terrible scourge of God directed against the sins of Islam and Christendom alike. Nor can he accept the more modern version that the whole thing is to be considered as a mighty natural explosion, terrifying and spontaneous like the awful thunderstorms of the late summer in Gobi.

Not only are there very good reasons why Chingis created the Mongol Empire and the army which swept through Asia, reasons arising directly out of the social life and history of the Mongols themselves, but an examination of these reasons, and analysis of that life, gives a true picture of the man and his times such as no amount of legend or anecdote can do. More than this, by placing the Mongol conquests in their true perspective in world history a remarkable light is thrown on the real relations between East and West, much that was formerly obscure becomes clear, and even the history of our own age grows more comprehensible.

The region about Lake Baikal has always been a cradle of peoples. It was from here that about the beginning of our era the Huns began their great westward migration, sweeping into Europe in the fourth century and leaving behind them the germs of new nations when the tide at last receded. In the sixth century the great kingdoms of the Turks sprang from the same fertile source around Baikal, the district between the rivers Orkhon and Selenga, and their western Empire received the ambassadors of the Emperor Justinian. The Turks were the last great wave to flow over Asia before the Mongols, yet the Huns, the Turks, the Mongols, only represent the highest points in a process continually taking place in Eastern and Central Asia. In China one after another the nomad armies sweep over the defences of the Middle Kingdom, founding dynasties or winning rich booty and high command. Persia and the Central Asian lands of the Caliphate are equally exposed. The struggle between the desert and the sown is the central feature of Asiatic history.

What is the secret of this furious struggle that is waged from the very beginning of Asiatic civilization right down to the period of its decline? No easy reference to climatic conditions, desiccation and so forth, can explain it. The numbers involved, even when whole peoples moved, were not so large that they had to travel continents to find pasture. It is only recently that the annual migrations of the Mongols have been carefully studied and mapped. The longest migration in the yearly cycle is well under 300 kilometres. The average is about 150. To travel immense distances in search of pasture is not only difficult, it is against all nomad traditions, nor is it necessary for them in order to maintain their herds.

The secret lies elsewhere, in the nature of their life and their social organization. The Huns, the Turks, the Mongols were all pastoral peoples, but to imagine either that they did or could live solely by their pastoral economy is far from the reality. They had need of many things which only townsmen and agriculturists could give them, metal work and arms of all kinds, clothes, carpets, embroideries, household utensils, even corn, for it is far from certain that they did not eat bread. Certainly many Turko-Mongol tribes living within easy reach of corn-bearing lands did so.

They in turn furnished much of value to the towns of Central Asia and China, horses, sheep, meat, wool, furs and sometimes slaves. We read of certain tribes bringing their products at night to the banks of the Syr, leaving them there for the townsfolk to take away and coming back the next night to fetch what was left by the townsmen in exchange.[1] Regular markets existed all along the Chinese frontier for trade with the nomads.

It was the need for exchange that drove the nomads into constant contact with the towns. And since they were desperately poor and their life hard and insecure, they were never averse from making the exchange one-sided where possible. If it were possible to rob, they robbed. If their needs were too great for robbery, if their own social organization began to develop so that they became knit together into something like peoples, they made war.

Of the Huns we still know very little, but the Turks at least had grown beyond the stage of mere pastoral barbarians. While maintaining still their patriarchal, clan society, they had the beginnings of a feudal organization, their kings were more than tribal elders, they had vassal tribes under their jurisdiction and they adopted, in the last days of their power, a form of writing which has left lonely monuments in the great monoliths from the district of the Orkhon river, whereon they have told the history of their people. Justinian's ambassadors found the Turkish king living in very splendid state, surrounded by many evidences of luxury. The interest shown by the nomads in cultivating trade relations with Byzantium, their keen grasp of the political situation in Asia, prove that they were not the simple barbarians we are asked to believe.

The nomads were in continual conflict with the civilized regions on the circumference of the great steppe regions of High Asia because their conditions of life forced this form of exchange upon them. Contact with civilization they must have, once they had developed out of barbarism, and that contact could hardly be other than violent.

Other forces, operating from within the civilized states themselves, were also at work. Every period of anarchy and social decay in China interrupted the normal trade and invited attacks from the

[1] For an interesting account of the survival into our own day of this primitive form or exchange, see the paper by Miss E. J. Lindgren, 'North-Western Manchuria and the Reindeer Tungus,' *Geographical Journal*, June 1930.

nomads. Strong governments in a united China, on the other hand, feeling the need to dominate more securely the trade routes to the west, were apt to push out into the steppes, forcing the tent-dwellers to change their pastures and move westward also to seek easier conditions of existence. The success of the Great Wall policy first pushed the Huns westward. The Turkish power arose in the period of anarchy preceding the rise of the great T'ang dynasty in China. The Mongols built their empire when Chinese feudalism was in complete decay, divided between the Northern Kins and the southern or native Sung dynasty.

It is in fact a mistake to consider the history of the nomad peoples of Eastern Asia apart from that of China. They are both part of one peculiar historical development, bound together economically and politically, continually influencing one another socially and culturally.

Nor can the historian neglect the profound effects of these nomad invasions on world history. Particularly can it be said of the Mongols that having effected a revolution in their own country they cleared the way for an immense series of revolutions in Asia and Europe. The cavalry of this young feudal power for the first time in history created a real world market, an achievement the decaying feudalism of the East failed to profit by (and here the Mongols themselves must bear the responsibility for their own devastations) but which gave the impulse to a new civilization in the West that in the end was to conquer and devastate Asia more dreadfully than ever did the armies of Chingis.

The Mongol troopers were rough and brutal conquerors. They had little regard for the precious things they stole or destroyed. Yet they made West and East known to one another for the first time since the death of Alexander the Great. In the wake of the Mongols the knowledge of many things came to Europe from China, printing and navigation, to mention but two revolutionary developments in technique. The Polo family were only the first of innumerable merchants and missionaries to make the journey overland to China.

Modern capitalist civilization with its great industrial technique arose in Europe, while Asia continued to slumber in its medieval dirt and picturesqueness. This too was largely the work of the Mongols, who gave Europe the chance to enrich itself at the expense of the East, while depriving Asia of its last hope of an equal start in the race for the new civilization.

Time, however, brings its revenges, and history is the greatest of all ironists. To-day there is again feverish activity in the river valleys that drain Lake Baikal and on the steppes of Eastern Asia. Power stations and blast furnaces are rising in the traditional home of the Turko-Mongol peoples. A native Mongol government rules in the home lands of Temujin-Chingis, but it is a government of the arats, the Mongol shepherds and simple men whom he and his band of adventurer-knights so despised and treated so hardly. The blast furnaces, chemical works and power stations are across the frontier of the Russian people whom the Mongols trounced so soundly for their backwardness in the thirteenth century. But the Russian schools and universities have many Mongol students, a Mongol horseman commands an army of the Soviet Union in Central Asia, Mongol airman fly above the steppes and forest-covered hills of the Onon, Kerulen and Selenga valleys, above the vast spaces of the Gobi, and Mongol poets are writing new songs for their people in which the name of Temujin-Chingis, their founder and first leader, is not forgotten.

2. Temujin's Asia

JUST as there comes in the lives of most men and women a period when all joy, hope and confidence vanish and in their place remain only a continuous dull pain and self-violence, so the same thing is to be observed in the life of nations. Such a period in the history of Asia was the century from 1150–1250, the very time when feudal Europe was in the flower of its age. It was as though Asia had grown weary at last of the crime of life and no new force was at hand to give courage for a renewed struggle, to hold out hope of triumph or the reward of a new relationship between men which should promise something other than treachery, greed, cruelty, lust and defeat.

Even such a dull and unobservant historian as M. Henri Cordier seems to feel something of this when in his history of the Sung dynasty he writes: 'The history of China constantly repeats itself. A feeble sovereign, addicted to pleasure or made idiot from superstitions, sometimes by both, ministers who are incapable when they are not treacherous, all-powerful eunuchs. To the founders of dynasties, who are generally men remarkable for their military qualities which seem to have exhausted the strength of their race in the fight for supreme power, there succeed princes who are rapidly made effeminate through vice, who have only the faults of the ancestors whose virtues had made the glory of their families.' What is true of China is no less true of Asia as a whole in this period.

If we examine a little deeper than M. Cordier the picture is even more desolating. The court, the eunuchs, the generals and the emperors were but a tiny minority, though an important one. For the mass of people life was utterly insecure and horrible. The peasant and the slave were the most wretched as they were the most exploited of human beings. The fatalism of the Eastern peasant is in fact no more than the utter indifference to life of those who expect nothing but the worst from it.

Feudalism in the East had no monopoly of violence and brutality. The peasant rarely appears in the literature of the Middle Ages in Europe, but where he does, as in that unforgettable glimpse of poverty and wretchedness in the midst of the lovesick gaiety of the tale of Aucassin and Nicolette, his position is little if any better than that of his Eastern brother. Yet it would be as wrong to imagine that East and West were alike in their social structure, as to identify the art and literature of medieval China with those of Catholic Europe.

Europe in the twelfth century was still in its lusty age. The seeds of decay were present, but it would be long before they ripened. Asia was in many ways centuries ahead of Europe but it was also centuries to its final decay and doom. The Asiatic state, with its immense frontiers and weak communications, with its enormous economic demands for the maintenance of the great irrigation works, was never so stable as the most ephemeral of European states. The surplus product of the peasant and the surplus labour of the slave were squeezed out in ever-growing quantities in order to maintain the great apparatus of internal and external plunder. So we find in Asia from time to time that the whole economic basis of society collapses; for generations ruin and famine are the only history.

Trade between East and West trickled slowly along the great traditional routes, overland through Central Asia to the Black Sea, through Persia to the Gulf, through the Red Sea to the Mediterranean, or overland again through Tabriz to Armenia. War or conquest might hold up trade for a generation along one of these routes, while of direct contact between the merchants of Europe and the great countries of Asia there was none. The great commercial entrepots in Syria and on the Black Sea were the meeting-places of East and West. Except in war, none passed beyond them from either side.

The Arabs had been the first to develop a great commerce with China. Traders, travellers, geographers and scientists, authors of the earliest and best accounts of the East in our era, these nomads of genius penetrated everywhere. At Canton and Hangchow, in the cities of Central Asia and the Chinese interior, they throve vastly well, forming the closest contacts with the trading class of every country where they penetrated. The usurer, the great merchant, had become the most important figure in Asiatic life, advising kings and causing the downfall of empires. Together with the soldier he was also to prove one of the chief causes of the collapse of Asiatic civilization. In our story of the fantastic rise of the Mongol adventurer Temujin to the lordship of all Asia he will play no small part.

In Europe also great forces were at work. Henry II in England, Frederick Barbarossa in the Empire, had proved it was possible to fight the Church and to sketch the outlines of nations and great states. The towns and communes of England, France, Germany and Italy were becoming thriving islands of commerce and industry amid the stormy seas of contending armies and the bloody hatreds of the ever-recurring peasant jacqueries. The Crusades were strengthening the towns, teaching new arts of war to the soldiers, weakening the traditional enemy in Asia.

At the beginning of the thirteenth century, about the time that Temujin was proclaimed the Chingis-Khan of the Mongols, the handsome young merchant of Assisi Giovanni Bernardone fell ill of a fever and during the delirium the gay young merchant died while in his place there was born a saint, Francesco, in love with life and at war with the greed of his own class, who saw in the love of money the root of all evil. The little friars of St. Francis, the disciples of poverty, were essentially the product of the new towns. The Abbot Joachim had preached the end of the world a few years before, to which Richard Lion Heart, resting with his crusading robbers at Messina, had listened doubtfully.

But a change was at hand. The world was stirring with a change which meant one thing to St. Francis, the prince of beggars, and yet another to St. Dominic, the learned and courtly prelate, the scourge of the unhappy peasants of the Albigenses, the scholar and dialectician.

Asia was full of books and learning. Her universities, her great libraries, the splendid art of Buddhism and the historical le rning of the great Persian and Arabian men of letters, put her centuries ahead of Europe. In the year when Chingis marched to the frontiers of China the university of Paris banned the Latin translations of Aristotle and forbade the study of certain of his books altogether. There were but three universities, at Bologna, Paris and Oxford, in the whole continent, and they were young.

China at the close of the twelfth century was in full decline, political and social. The great T'ang dynasty had been succeeded during the tenth century by a long period of strife and confusion, that of the so-called five dynasties, till at last, in the middle of the century, the new dynasty of the Sung was established, to reign till the grandchildren of Chingis broke and destroyed them three hundred years later. The T'ang had been a brilliant dynasty. China under their rule was the greatest empire in the world and Chinese civilization reached such heights as no other country has ever surpassed. But the price was the ruin of the whole land and the misery of the people. The agony of the T'ang was accompanied by a terrible jacquerie that swept the country, murdering the merchants and the Arab traders, sacking Canton, a movement of such ferocious revenge that the Turkish horsemen were called in by the desperate emperors to protect them, in vain, against their own subjects.

The Sung changed nothing. The country under their rule grew ever more exhausted, till the very soil refused to yield the peasants their life's nourishment, drought and material disaster became almost a part of Chinese life. The famous reforms of Wan-An-Shi in the eleventh century held up the collapse for a little, but Wan-An-Shi was too wise for his generation and had no great social force to support him, while every general and official saw his position menaced by this statesman who wished to let the poor man breathe, even though the rich man he forced thereby to curtail a little his luxury. The very frontiers could no longer be defended. First the Turkish Khitans stormed the northern provinces, then they in turn yielded to the Tungusic Kin or 'golden' dynasty, the ancestors of the Manchus. The Sung ruled only south of the Yangtze. It was a divided China that faced the Mongols, a China whose two halves were always intriguing for the support of the restless nomad fringe.

The trade routes from China to the West were no less disturbed throughout the twelfth century. The Khitans, driven out of Northern China by the Manchurian Kin, or Jurjens, built a new empire for themselves in Central Asia. Their centre was in the lands of the Uighur and in Eastern Turkestan, but their conquests spread at one time as far west as Bokhara and Samarkand, the two great homes of Central Asian trade and Islamic culture. Their empire was known as Kara-Khitai, the empire of Black Cathay. Another kingdom, that of Hsi-Hsia, inhabited by the Tibetan Tangut or Hsia, held the debouches into China proper, the ancient caravan road through the Lop Nor region. The Tangut kingdom lived and thrived on the divisions between the Chinese people, forming a handy refuge for every rebel against the Chinese state, in seditious league with the never-ending peasant movements, at all times a nest of hardy soldiers and desperate fugitives.

Both these states, though they were unstable and weak, founded and maintained by military conquest, were centres of ancient culture. Their walled cities contained Buddhist temples and libraries, Nestorian churches and Mohammedan mosques. The glorious reds and blues of Buddhist art made a blaze of colour on the walls of the temples or the sacred grottoes. In the gracious figures of these paintings the fine features of Iranians, the descendants of Manichæan missionaries, the draperies and athletic beauty of Greek art, the heritage of Alexander's great campaign, were mingled with the purely Chinese. No doubt by this time the red-robed monks and priests who served in the temples had lost most traces of the great Buddhist culture which produced these paintings. Most of them, like the priests whom the sage Ch'ang Ch'un addressed, were probably illiterate. To their Moslem subjects, these Kara-Khitan conquerors with their train of Tangut and Uighur followers, were merely ignorant idol-worshippers.

In Central Asia and Persia (Iran), the twelfth century was also one of political decay and social unrest. The Turkoman conquerors who had founded the Seljukid empire, which at the height of its glory stretched from the Black Sea to the Persian Gulf and eastward to the banks of the Oxus, reduced the Caliph of Baghdad to the mere spiritual head of Islam. They themselves, copying their Christian rivals in Europe, created a great secular power ruled by the 'Sultan of Islam,' who corresponded to the Holy Roman Emperor.

It would be a mistake, however, to see the Seljukid Empire, or any of the great Asiatic states as a centralized monarchy. According to Turkish clan law, different members of the family ruled different parts of the empire, almost as independent states. Though there was but one Sultan of Islam, there were many Seljukid sultans. During the century a successful rival to the Seljukids arose in Khwarizmia, the modern Khiva, whose viceroys, the Khwarizm-Shahs, conquered first the central Asian states of the Seljuks, and finally, by the beginning of the thirteenth century, were masters of Iran and Irak as well. The ruler of this new empire of the West, when it first came into contact with Chingis-Khan, was a certain Mohammed-ben-Takash, the Khawrizm-Shah and reigning Sultan of Islam. A narrow, but greedy, vain and ambitious man, his eyes were turned eastward, towards the turbulent countries of Kara-Khitai and Hsi-Hsia, with the aim of monopolizing all the rich commerce that passed along the great Khorasan high road and thence through the basins of the Ili and the Tarim rivers to the busy cities of China.

To understand the peculiar character of Asiatic history, the causes of its political instability, the real root of that Asiatic pessimism, miscalled fatalism, which has placed such a distinguishing mark on the civilization of the continent, we must go deeper than a mere description of the political divisions in the period which interests us. The very idea of change, in the form of enrichment, of concentration (in the chemical sense) which is the basis of the Western view of life, is foreign and incomprehensible to the Asiatic. He thinks always in terms of renewal, of the eternal return to the starting-point in order that the cycle of life may begin afresh.

When you ride over the steppes and plains of Central Asia, an islander from the North Sea, you are assailed by the strangest, most contradictory emotions until you become used to the vast distances. At first you feel overwhelmed by the feeling of land, that here you are in the driest, most continental and essentially land parts of the world. The sea becomes a distant dream; so many thousands of miles away in this or that direction—you are equidistant from all the great oceans, as near to the Atlantic as to the Pacific. And then, when, choked with dust and blinded by the monotonous glare of yellow earth, brilliant sky and bright sun, you have at last forgotten the very existence of sea, you are suddenly seized by the feeling that you are riding by the shores of a great ocean. That long purple-brown cliff which stretches to your left must surely have the waves beating at its foot.

There is an explanation for this. The centre of Asia in prehistoric times was filled by a vast inland sea. The cliff whose sharp outline caught your attention contains sea fossils in its crumbling, gravelly clay. The natural history of Asia is a history of desiccation, of the gradual drying up of vast areas till only the unnatural pools of the Caspian and Aral salt-lakes are left now in this desert of land.

The causes of this desiccation, which continues throughout historical times, are to be found in the mighty ranges of mountains which cut across Asia from north to south, the ranges of the far Siberian north, the Atlai, the Tien Shan, the Himalaya and the Hindu Kush. The changes in the glacial life of these snow-clad giants have altered the face of a great part of the earth. The drying-up of Asia has also given a peculiar stamp to the life of its human population.

Two features stand out, the great rivers, and the vast expanses of steppe. Around these features in historical times men began to live in two different ways: in the oases, along the river valleys, they lived a settled life in towns and villages, tilling the earth, producing and manufacturing; on the steppe they lived a pastoral, nomad life. This conflict of two economies, those of 'the desert' and 'the sown,' has been the central feature of Asiatic history, determining its peculiar course. Because of it, struggles between classes and nations have in Asia assumed a different form and gone a different way from the way of Europe and the West.

The two economies, as each developed to civilized life, could not exist independently of one another. They must meet, exchange and conflict. It would be wrong to regard the nomad way of life as barbarous. The earliest civilizations in Northern Asia were nomadic and the steppe culture of Siberia, carried into China, helped to build the greatest of all the settled civilizations of Asia. We know to-day that the nomad Scythians were also far from being barbarians, that they gave much to all the settled peoples with whom they came in contact.

But the nomad life could not remain self-contained and self-sufficient. It is a poor life and a hard one by its very nature. The Chinese poets loved to compare the free and happy horseman of the grassy plains, riding with his hunting eagle on his wrist, with the luxury and contradictions of their own court life. But at the beginning of this book I placed deliberately another and a truer image, that of the frozen, horseless, ragged, enduring nomad alone against the cruelty of the elements. There is a Turkish proverb, 'the steppe is wide and heaven is far,' which sums up exactly the real position.

The deserts are sandy and waterless, burning hot in summer and freezing in winter. The grass lands are torn by mighty winds, lashed by storms, frozen in winter also. In midsummer the grass is brown and dry, useless for man or beast. The burning summer is a very brief one, the thunderstorms of August heralding the grey cold autumn which begins in September. Then there may come a brief Indian summer, the best time of the year, when the cool dry air is sun-warmed and kind, keen and quick to the blood. As for winter, with its great frosts and bitter winds against which there is no protection, it is only a torment to those who must live through it.

The people live by their beasts alone, the sheep, cattle, horses and, in some places, camels. The animals are not always as hardy as the men and women. Many of them die on the winter pastures. The horse, the small, sturdy, shaggy Mongolian pony, is the best loved and most important of the nomad's possessions. The mare gives him milk, the *kumys* which is the national drink, a sharp, sour, bluish-whitish liquid, which has great properties of strength-giving and is not to be despised after a long day's ride by the most finicking European. On his pacer the nomad can ride untired for days on end, master of the great distances of the steppe. The stages of nomad history are connected with the horse, with the invention of the bridle and then, much later, of the stirrup, which gave the nomad fighter the chance to wield his deadly lance and shoot accurately from the saddle with the bow, so that he became the most effective and dreaded cavalryman in the world. From the ability to fight and manœuvre in mass given him by the stirrup, arose the need for military leaders, and with these leaders developed the nomad feudalism that reached its highest point under the Mongol Chingis-Khan.

Imagine him then, this typical rider of the steppe, short, round-skulled, big-boned and sturdy, the brown eyes set just above the high cheek-bones and reddened with exposure and grit, the unwieldy carriage that of a man always in the saddle, his dress a long coat of brown, coarse cloth, girded across the middle, the sleeves wide and long, his cap of fox-skin or of white felt embroidered in red and blue wool. The hair on his face is sparse, but he has something of a beard, while his head is unshaven, the wiry black hair bound into two plaits. His teeth are dazzling white and he is cheerful and friendly enough in company, though inclined to long periods of gloomy moroseness.

He eats mutton, loves gluttonous feasting and heavy drinking, but can do so only very rarely, owing to his poverty. In the early summer, however, when the worst is over with the breeding of his flocks, when the mares are giving milk freely and the grass is still fresh and green, he goes to the clan meeting, to the wrestling and races, where a feast is held, horses are killed, and for a brief moment he knows satisfaction and plenty.

Crossing the steppe is an art—like navigation without instruments. He knows his position partly from memory, the astonishing nomad memory that knows the position of every stone and carries the shape of the country in mind as true as a photograph, partly, at night, by the stars, or again by the flight of the cranes or wild geese urgent across the blue sky. The sky is his supreme spirit, his God. But the winds, the stones, the rivers, the forests, all have their spirits, mostly evil. The *shaman*, the medicine-man, can commune with them and is, if not the master of nature, at least its confidant. Life is a constant battle, against spirits and against man. His own spirit is as hardy and fearless as his rough life compels him to be and he is as indifferent to suffering in others as in himself. His speech is poetry, for he does not know writing and poetry is the easiest way of communicating his thoughts. He sings the past of his race, the great Khans of the Huns and the Turks, the joy of battle, the skill and pleasure of the hunt, the beauty of his quiet, dark-eyed, light-skinned women. His speech and song are full of images from the life of the steppe, the birds, the wild animals, the carts which bear his tents, his horses, his weapons, and he knows no other, for his imagination, like his life, is bounded by these.

His way of life at the time of which we write was rougher, his society more democratic and less corrupt than that of the towns, and his military skill infinitely higher than that of the settled peoples with whom he was constantly at war. Racially the nomad of Central and Eastern Asia was little different from the townsman. By our era no such thing as a purely nomadic race was left. The Iranian (Persian) population had been settled on the land and in the towns for over a thousand years. The Turanian peoples (Turks) were fairly divided. Many kept their old life and traditions, but a good half were settled, and even the Mongols, whom we think of as purely nomadic, had whole tribes living a settled existence near the Great Wall of China.

The towns of Asia, rising as military camps and trading posts, had become great and beautiful cities, the marvel of the civilized world. The streets of their bazaars were filled with the booths of busy craftsmen of all kinds, they were splendid with their tiled mosques and colleges, their fountains and shady ponds, beautiful with green gardens and orchards. The social life of these settled states was, however, entirely conditioned by this strange dual economy of the continent.

Any development among the nomads had its immediate effect on the great states. A temporary unification of the tribes was always followed by an invasion of the settled countries, their conquest, and the establishment of a nomad dynasty and a new feudal ruling class. The aim of the new rulers was the plunder of the population. To strengthen themselves they built up armies from the tribes, often slave armies, quite apart from the people. With their own assimilation by the higher culture which they had conquered came their degeneration and decay, together with that of their armies, and inevitable conquest by a fresh invader from the steppe.

The wealthy towns sometimes sought freedom from this yoke by becoming free republics under a merchant oligarchy, as in Italy. But this never lasted long enough to ensure the supremacy of the merchant class. Either the oligarchy became a tyranny, as in Bokhara and Samarkand, or else it gave way in time to a stronger nomad conqueror. There were no nations and no national forces. Classes there were, and between the classes a bitter unending struggle, a struggle which could never end in the enrichment of life, in the smelting of a new society, but only in destruction and renewal. Ibn Haldun, the great Arab philosopher, when he wished to describe the societies of Asia used the image of an Arab poet—they were 'like silkworms which weave a cocoon that they might die in it.' The pessimism engendered by history is expressed by yet another Arab poet. 'The end is like unto the beginning—morning and evening—one and the same miracle.'

This then was Asia at the time of the birth of Temujin: in science, in art, in philosophy and literature, in the size and grandeur of its towns, the wonder of its libraries and unversities, centuries ahead of Europe. Yet it was a society in which nothing was firm and stable, in which the very poets and philosophers could only mourn the beauty of passing things and seek comfort in a mystic communion with an absolute spirit outside of the agony of life, a society where every man was at war with his brother, in which cruelty, violence and oppression were the laws of being. States and empires rose and vanished on the immense steppe, their very names unknown in the West. Only the legend of the immense wealth of Asia was constant in the imagination of the youthful peoples of Europe, so that when a petty Tatar princeling adopted the Nestorian heresy the fame of it spread to the courts of Europe and the forged letter of Prester John awakened men's greed as well as their religious instincts with the fabulous story of the riches of this illiterate nomad and the great state of his equally fabulous court.

3. The Land and the People

BAIKAL is one of the most beautiful lakes in the world. The high bluffs, forest-crowned, the swift rivers which drain from and into its blue depths, the mists that cover the wide waters, the quick, invigorating air, the solitude and quiet, all fit it to be the breast which has given suck to so many heroic peoples. East of Baikal the country becomes broken steppe again, then come mountains, and a fresh series of swift-running streams to form the headwaters of the Amur. By one of these rivers, the Onon, Temujin-Chingis was born.

But if Baikal itself and the country to the east is hilly, forested and intersected by rivers and streams, to the south the land grows flatter and drier. The fringes of Mongolia proper are great grass plains, green in spring, grey-blue in summer and grey-brown in winter. Here the rivers are rarer, wider and slower, the only trees a few ancient elms in their valleys. Further south again is the Gobi, a great desert of dust, and dry, yellow, gravelly clay. Here and there are stretches of sand and rolling dunes. There are many lakes, most of them salt, and the only vegetation is tamarisk, camel shrub and thorn. The desert is not flat but wind-eroded into fantastic, card-board shapes, like those studio sets German producers made for their macabre fantasy films in the early days of the 'artistic' film.

Mongolia and the Mongols can in no way be compared to that other great land of a nomad people, Arabia. The climatic conditions are far more varied, the economic life quite different. The Arab has little more than his horses, sheep and camels. The Mongol and the Turkish nomads have also abundance of cattle, sheep and goats. They have close at hand well-watered country and rich pastures, they have on their lands minerals and wide areas suitable for settled cultivation. From time to time one or other of these Turko-Mongol peoples has in fact settled down, and, though their life has been a continual struggle with their nomad brothers, they have even built up rich and splendid civilizations. The winter in Mongolia is long and harsh, the summer brief, hot and thundery.

Like the Arabs, the Mongols were placed by nature on a great trade route, and it is this fact above all which has played an overwhelming part in their history, as it has also caused them to play a part no less important in the history of other peoples.

All the vast central area of Asia has from the most ancient times been inhabited by nomad peoples, living in round felt tents, eating meat and drinking the milk of mares. At the beginning of our era the single original of all these nations had split into three main branches, the Turks, the Tunguses and the Mongols, each with their own language and their own peculiarities of social life, but maintaining the same ethnical characteristics, the same kind of social organization and mode of life. It has been suggested that the roots of these three divisions go back to a primitive division of labour. At least it is certain that the Tunguses began to develop primarily as fishers and hunters inhabiting the vast forest regions of East Siberia, that the Mongols became nomad herders of horses and sheep and that the Turks early began to work iron and to till the earth as well as to pasture their herds.

It may be that from this original, primitive Turko-Mongol people there survived into historical times at least one important fragment, the Uighurs. Certainly the Uighurs were the earliest iron-workers, perhaps the earliest agriculturists and always the most advanced and capable of all these peoples. They played a great part in the Turkish confederacy of the sixth and seventh centuries, and it may be that they were the geniuses to adopt the Runic alphabet in which the first monuments of the Turkish language were written on the great monoliths that lie by the Orkhon and Selenga rivers. Certainly, when their own empire succeeded that of the Turks, in the eighth century, they created a great civilization and, through the medium of the Soghdian alphabet, the first Turkish literature.

So stable was the Uighur culture that conquest could not destroy it. Uighur merchants rivalled the Uzbeks from Tashkent and Samarkand for the monopoly of the nomad trade in Easter Asia all through the early Middle Ages. As we shall see, they played a great part in the building of the Empire of Chingis. On the frontiers of China and Soviet Asia to this day there exist people who bear the proud name of Uighur. You may even meet tall youths on the Moscow boulevard by the Eastern University, fox-skin caps covering their close-cropped heads as the only outward relic of Asia, who claim the name of

Uighur and are very conscious of their great past.

To go back farther than this proto-race of the three great divisions is a hazardous task. We do know, however, that this part of the world was once inhabited by a race which conquered China, exterminating its aboriginal population, a race with white skins and fair hair, which later mixed with the original Turko-Mongol peoples. A Russian archæologist, Grumm-Brizhimailo, has professed to have found traces of this race among Mongols, Kirghiz and Uighurs, and in certain physical peculiarities of Chingis, his blue eyes, his great stature and his long beard, he claims there is proof that he too had this ancient blood in his veins. But we may safely leave these ancient Din-lins, as they are called, to their unknown fate. There are more explanations than one to account for blue eyes, as many a harassed parent has discovered, and for our purpose it is enough to say that the Mongols are the last of a series of peoples to develop from this dead heart of Asia, where it is now believed that the first man had his home.

The Mongols themselves were only a clan of the people we now term Mongol, a clan without a history till the beginning of the twelfth century when we first hear of their chief Kabul-Khan raising a rebellion against the Kin emperors of China. Like all the Turko-Mongol peoples they trace their own legendary origin back to a wolf, and from the sixth to the twelfth century seem to have pastured their herds by the headwaters of the Onon and on the plains where now live the Khalka Mongols of the Republic of Outer Mongolia.

If the Mongols had as yet made no appearance in history, this does not allow us to make the easy assumption that they had known none. The historians have so far contented themselves with telling us about these great nomad nations, Huns, Turks, Mongols, that they lived in tents, had a pastoral economy, patriarchal family relations and that in search of suitable pasture lands, as their own country became desiccated, they conquered at one time or another, most of the world. For the rest, the historians are content to tell us who was conquered, and where, and when, who were the rulers of these great nomad empires, and what traces they left behind them among the conquered. But this is not history. It is not even good anecdote. The social organization of these peoples was the result of long and complex development. To tell us that they lived in tents and ate meat explains no more than to say that the medieval serf lived in a hut and ate bread, when he could get it. And marvellous indeed must have been the appetites of those few thousand head of horses and sheep that had to roam from Baikal to the plains of Hungary before they found satisfaction. Indeed, we know that in historic times there has been no great desiccation of middle and High Asia, and to explain the great invasions we must look for the cause in the life of these peoples itself, in that history which is supposed not to exist.

The Mongols had two main divisions, those who lived in the forest by hunting and trapping, and those who lived on the steppe in nomadic communities. The Chinese called the former 'wild' Tatars, the latter the 'black,' and added a third category, the 'white' Tatars who lived near the Great Wall under Chinese influence, and knew town life. The clan of the Borjigin, which gave birth to Temujin, was part of the great Mongol Taijiut tribe, living in the region of the Onon and the Kerulen, on the border between the forest and the steppe, with many characteristics of both 'wild' and 'black' Tatars, though predominantly nomads of the steppe.

To their civilized neighbours the Turks and Mongols always appeared to live a free and happy life on the wide expanses of the steppe, in that invigorating air. Free they were not, their very wanderings being bound by rules as strict as those of the most complicated city life, and as for happiness, it is a word usually closer to the desire of him who uses it than to the object to which it is applied. The nomads pastured sheep, cattle, goats and horses. Camels at that time were rare among the Mongols, while between the clans who herded sheep and the horse breeders there was a division, the latter being the aristocrats of the steppe.[1] The same pastures did not suit both and the horsemen despised the shepherds.

In each season of the year, spring, summer, autumn and winter, the nomad has a different pasture to which he moves with his flocks, his half-wild dogs, his beehive tents and his women. The length of the journey and the character of the halting place vary according to the nature of the country. In modern Mongolia, in the Ubur-Hangai district, a typical nomad cycle is very great in distance, 150–200 kilometres, and the pastures vary greatly in character. In summer the tents are pitched by the swift currents of the rivers, while they winter far away to the south, among the lakes, almost in the Gobi-Altai.

[1] The same division exists to this day in the United States, where the cowboy despises the shepherd.

In summer the cool hills and the tumbling rivers with their rain-water and rich valleys are used, in winter the low grounds of the Gobi where there is no snow, a late winter and early spring. Autumn and spring are taken up by numerous and temporary halts in the journey between the two main pasture grounds. In other parts of the country the reverse is the way, to winter on the southern slopes of the hills, using snow in place of water, and to spend the summer on the low-lying steppes, near to water.

The famous beehive tent, made of felts hung round a trellis work of osier, was the creation of this nomad life, and its centre. Easily erected or dismantled, it is a splendid protection against the harsh weather of the Asian steppes, well-ventilated, roomy, and warm in winter and cool in summer. Its shape is such that without ropes or pegs it can withstand the rush of the mighty winds. The average tent is perhaps some twenty feet across, but they vary greatly. The Turkish Khan received Justinian's ambassadors in a great tent like a palace, with rich hangings and carven furniture. The Mongols carried their tents on bullock-carts (kibitkas), which enabled them to move camp with the greatest rapidity on the approach of an enemy. To-day the very memory of these carts has gone from the Mongol people, though the tents themselves remain unchanged.

The old tribal society went from pasture to pasture in great companies of several hundred tents, forming up in a wide circle at the end of each march. Such a circular camp of tents the Mongols called *guriyen* or *kuren*, but in Chingis' day this form of wandering had already given way to a new organization, expressive of the changes taking place among the Mongols themselves. The *guriyen* remained as a military formation only.

For generations a class of rich and aristocratic clan leaders had been growing up, owners of great herds of cattle and horses. For them it was no profit to travel in the clumsy *guriyen*. They preferred to go off alone in the *ayil*, as the small companies of one family or group of families were known. But to travel thus, in small companies with great herds, was to invite danger, as Professor Vladimirtsov has shown. The great *guriyen* was broken up into small ones, in which the rich lords lived for protection, while their men pastured their herds in the *ayils*.

The herds were not large. A flock of 1,000 sheep belonging to an Uzbek merchant calls for special mention in the *Secret History*. So life was not easy, and food could get dangerously scarce. Large herds are to-day looked on by the Mongols as a kind of insurance against disaster. In the twelfth century that insurance was little developed. To live on their herds alone was impossible for the Mongols and they had to supplement their food supply. This they did by hunting.

Hunting was not only an important economic and social function, it was the whole poetry of the nomad life. Their speech is full of metaphors of the hunt. The generals of Chingis are likened to hunting dogs and hawks by their enemies. 'Wherein lies the joy and triumph of men?' Chingis asked Burji-noyon, his chief prince. And Burji answered: 'It lies in a man taking on his wrist his bluehawk which has been fed on flesh and mewed its feathers in winter, and, seated on a goodly, well-fed gelding, to hunt in the early spring after the blue-headed birds, and also to dress in goodly clothes and garments.' To this question yet another chief answered: 'Delight is to be found when beasts, like gerfalcons, swoop upon cranes, dash them from the air with their claws and seize them.' And though Chingis told them: 'You have not answered well,' they had answered as their hearts told them.

He himself, in the days of his poverty, was reduced to hunting the prairie mice in order to keep alive.

The Mongols also used corn to some extent, importing it from the Kirghiz of the Yenesei, through the Muslim merchants who controlled the grain trade. But their chief food, then as now, was mutton and they drank the milk of mares, fermented by churning in skins, *kumys* as it is called.

At one time, early in our era, it is clear that the Mongols were considerable craftsmen in bronze and iron, apt at making all kinds of vessels and weapons from wood, and potters also. By the twelfth century these arts had almost died out amongst them and they imported most made things. Carpenters and smiths still held an honoured place in their society, but this military nation had nevertheless to import even its weapons from other lands, from China and from Khorasan in the first place. Bows and arrows, cavalry lances, they made themselves, other parts of their equipment also, for that matter, but as soon as they began to make war on a large scale their slender productive resources failed them and they were forced to rely on other countries for their weapons.

In the twelfth century, as to-day, these Mongol and Turkish tribes lived upon one of the great land-routes to China. This had long ago had the effect of breaking up their old self-sufficient clan life.

Crafts had declined, Uighur and Uzbek merchants had developed a considerable trade among the nomads, money had doubtless appeared, though most of the trade was by simple exchange, and subsidies from the Chinese emperors to the clan and tribal leaders had all assisted in creating a powerful aristocracy. Even towns were common enough on the caravan routes and in the regions near the Great Wall. Probably none of the Mongol tribes themselves ever built towns or settled permanently in them before the rise of Chingis-Khan's great empire, but many of them must nevertheless have been well acquainted with town-life.

The steppe-town of those days was half trading-station and half nomad encampment. A Nestorian church or Buddhist monastery, a Chinese quarter, a few houses or inns where the merchants, Uighur or Uzbek, quartered, and then the nomad tents, which might be here to-day and gone to-morrow, were their chief features. Perhaps the land around the town was irrigated and cultivated, sometimes by Mongols, more often by Turks. The great religious foundations, Nestorian or Buddhist, were deeply interested in trade and often great landowners as well as money-lenders and bankers. The explorations of such travellers as Sir Aurel Stein and Owen Lattimore have helped to give us such a picture of these frontier trading-towns, but in fact the same kind of settlement can still be observed all over Central Asia and the Far East, the only difference being in the lesser part played to-day by the religious foundations. The town is above all a trading-centre and its permanent inhabitants generally of alien race.

Yet when we speak of wealth and possessions among the Mongols of the twelfth century the term must be a very limited and relative one. Goods of all kinds were unbelievably scarce. The young Temujin when his wife brought him a sable coat as dowry, acquired thereby a wealth that proved his salvation and in a sense was the foundation of his fortune. The Mongol of to-day who owns but twenty head of horses and cattle of all kinds is considered a poor man. But the great Temujin had only eight geldings and one horse for all his family in the days of his poverty, despite his noble birth.

The basis of Mongol society was the patriarchal clan, the *obog*, which in turn was divided into families, 'bones,' or *yasun* in the Mongol terminology. The clan did not permit inter-marriage among its members and the young men had to seek their wives outside the clan. The young Temujin was thus betrothed as a child to a maiden of the Olhonod tribe, who pitched their tents far away to the south of the pastures of his own clan, in the very Gobi, beyond the river Kerulen. As in all societies where such marriage customs prevail the difficulty of finding a wife within the permitted clans was great and led to constant raiding and kidnapping, with consequent blood-feuds. Temujin was to suffer himself the terrible results of such a rape and blood-feud. His father Yesugei stole his wife from the Merkits and they in turn years later raided the camp of Temujin and stole his young bride.

There was no common property among the Mongols. Each *ayil*, or nomad household, held its own sheep and herds, its own tents and gear. On the death of the father his tent (*yurt*) and wives with all their property passed to the youngest son, the 'lord of the hearth and yurt.' As each child married he received his own *ayil*, tents, horses and flocks, and share in the grazing-grounds, all that is, save the youngest who remained in the *ayil* of the father till the latter's death. When a man died leaving his children still in infancy, the widow assumed all the rights of her husband, including even the leadership of the clan or tribe, until such time as her children grew to manhood and married. Among both Mongols and Turks the position of the widow was of great importance. In some cases she might become the ruler of a great empire.

The women played a part of great importance in this nomad life. They were the producers, making almost everything that was needed, while the men confined themselves in most cases to hunting and to caring for the flocks. The latter was no light task, by the way, and called for great knowledge, endurance and skill. Each wife had a right to her own tent and household and it was usual for them to follow their husbands to war. In war also the women played their part, for they had much to do in caring for the men's gear, in preparing food and tending the flocks while their men fought.

The clan was also a religious unit. The rude pantheism and nature worship of the nomads was bound up with the life of the clan and the making of sacrifices in its name. The *shaman* or witch-doctor, played no great part among the steppe-dwellers, for his power was the greatest in the forests, where he was often the ruler as well as priest. To be allowed to take part in the offering of sacrifices meant that one had full rights as a member of the clan. To be excluded was equivalent to expulsion from it and to being driven out to starvation or outlawry in the steppe. The Mongols did not believe in any god, but in the spirits of nature and the mighty power of the Blue Sky, with its angry storms and burning sun, its brilliant stars at night.

Within this strange society many great changes were taking place in the years before the birth of Temujin. This was no free and happy community, living without care as its fathers had lived for centuries before. From Chingis himself we know that he found his people living in anarchy and disorder, amid every sign of the decay of their society. The great Persian historian Rashid ed-Din has reported his words. 'The children no longer hearkened to the good words of their fathers. The younger brothers did not heed the words of the elder brothers. Husbands did not trust their wives and the wives did not obey the commands of their husbands. . . . The wealthy did not help the rulers to grow powerful and strong. For this reason there were many in opposition, there were thieves, liars, rebels and robbers. The sun did not appear to such a people in their dwelling-places, that is to say, they stole, and their horses and herds had no peace. The horses they rode in the van were given no rest and so inevitably these horses died, were worn out, grew rotten and were destroyed. Such was this tribe without order and without sense.'

Among these tribes murder, rape and theft were the normal way of life. They knew rich and poor, lord and vassal, master and slave. The disorder and anarchy condemned by their great emperor were the result of the decay of the old patriarchal society among the Mongols and the gradual growth within it of new relationships which Professor Vladimirtsov has quite justly termed 'nomad feudalism.'

The old clans with their unbroken blood relationships had long ago split up and dispersed, and this for two reasons. First, because certain families had voluntarily broken away, forming new clans and seeking new pastures. Second, because when a clan was defeated in war, its members were broken up and enslaved. The institution of vassal clans was almost universal among the Mongols, so that every important tribe or clan had its own vassals formed of other clans or fragments of clans. Such tribes or clans were known as *unagan bogol*. They went from pasture to pasture with their lords, and they themselves were as complex a social organization as the aristocratic tribes to whom they owed allegiance. Their chief would even marry into the suzerain's family. Yet another kind of dependant were the *inje*, the young men who came into the clan as part of a bride's dowry. Lastly there were the simple slaves, known by a word meaning 'brave lads,' quick and clever in menial work at the great hunts, as shepherds and stable-boys.

The aristocracy were the blood members of the clan, though they too included both rich and poor, influential or insignificant members. So among the Mongols there was a ruling class of wealthy aristocrats, heads of the clan or tribe, whether a free clan or a vassal clan, then the poor folk of the free and vassal clans, and lastly the slaves, the 'brave lads.' To the great lords went all the spoils of the chase, and therefore the richest products of their nomad economy in the shape of precious skins and furs. In war also theirs was the first choice of all the booty. But in addition it is clear that they received many feudal services from their vassals. Some families had to perform the task of churning the *kumys* (mare's milk) for the great families, other poor people had to go to the rich families at the sheep-shearing, and these, of course, were generally women since the work of the men, vassal or free, was ever among the horses and flocks out in the steppe, herding and tending.

Yet this is not sufficient to explain the anarchy which so angered Chingis and which he gave his later life to ending. The actual breaking up of the clan itself through the enrichment and voluntary secession of its stronger members was the cause of this. We have seen that the old way of life in the *guriyen*, the great nomad procession of carts and tents of a whole clan, had given place to the *ayil*, the smaller nomad unit of the important family. But the division went further than this. As each head of a family grew rich in flocks and followers he split away from the clan to form a new clan, with its own vassals, serving-men and slaves, its own military organization for protection and for raiding.

Temujin's own father was such a nomad leader. Yesugei-Bagatur broke away from the parent clan of Borjigin and gathered about him his own followers and vassals, his relatives and their men. He organized his companionship of free men-at-arms, esquires, raided the neighbouring tribe of Tatars with whom he was at blood-feud, captured one of their chiefs, stole himself a wife from another man, betrothed his son and sealed the match with the gift of a stallion, was turbulently proud of his descent from the aristocratic Borjigins and became sworn brother (*anda*) to the Khan of the neighbouring Keraits, Togrul, who was later to play a great part in the life of his son. Yesugei was just such a little lord as sprang up in thousands in Europe, in the early days of feudalism, half a robber and half an aristocrat, beggarly and proud.

Such lords were known as *noyon*, 'prince,' among the Mongols. They were the cause of the turmoil of the nomad life, its insecurity and its dark crimes and hatreds. Each sought to attract as many followers as he could, to subdue others and make them his vassals or slaves, to build a military force with any bold spirits who would follow his horse-tail banner. The greater the number of military followers, the more numerous the wealthy vassals, then the larger the number of mouths dependent on the bounty of this lord of the steppe. A generous lord had many followers, a weak or unsuccessful one soon had none. So the prince or tribal leader had continually to bestir himself to keep his rude following in plenty, to get for them the best pastures and the best hunting-grounds, to make the lordliest presents. To him for protection came the weak and the defeated and one by one the old blood clans became dispersed, intermingled and scattered, though their names remained. The rude democracy of their early life became only a memory, the rule of the strongest the only law, and the lands of the Mongols the scene of constant turmoil and fighting.

Europe had passed through the same stage of feudal formation two centuries before, though Europe was a land of agricultural communities and not of nomad pastoralists. Clearly the time was coming among the Mongols when one lord must beat the others, shatter the last fragments of the old patriarchal life and build a new one on the basis of the new relationships. Temujin-Chingis was born at a time of crisis among his own people when all was ready for the leader who should build the new society. It was his fate also to be born when the two great feudal states on either side of him, the Khwarizmian Empire in Central Asia and the Kin Empire in China, were in full decay. It was this combination which made it the destiny of the Mongol nomad to become the Emperor of the world, the greatest conqueror since Alexander the godlike, prince of Macedon.

PART II

Genghis Khan

1. The Eagle Mews its Feathers

THE names of the rivers are music—Onon, Selenga, Ingoda, Kerulen, Tula, and they run through the narrow valleys with their waving trees and across the level steppes. Tribes of two races lived on the lands they watered—the Tatars,[1] whom men later called Mongols, and the Turks. The Tatars or Mongols were divided into Merkits, who dwelled in the forests near Baikal, the Kongirat and the Taijiut, while the chief peoples among the Turks were the Kerait who dwelled between the Orkhon and the Great Wall, and the Naiman whose lands were in the rich region between the Orkhon and the Altai mountains. Since 1009 the Kerait were Christians, converted by the Nestorian bishop of Merv in Central Asia, while among the Naiman pagan shamanists and Christian priests alike were to be found. The Kerait were much mixed with the Mongols and spoke the Mongol tongue.

The Borjigin were an ancient clan of the Taijiut, aristocrats of the steppe. Their leader Kabul Khan in the early years of the twelfth century gave his people renown and united many tribes under his leadership in one *ulus* or confederation. Kabul Khan, no doubt with a subsidy from the Chinese Southern or Sung dynasty, made forays into China against the armies of the northern Kin emperors. He was a drunken, rough barbarian and liked to recall how he pulled the beard of the grave Kin monarch when they met to make peace. The Kin was buying the nomad's support and affected to overlook the insult but he sought later to seize Kabul by treachery. The Mongol, however, was too cunning for him, and repaid treachery by deeper treachery, slaying the Chinese ambassadors.

The Tatars, in the pay of the Kin, made war on the Borjigin after Kabul's death and seizing two of their chiefs handed them over

[1] Tatar was the name of a Mongol tribe, the hereditary enemies of the Mongol clan of Borjigin.

to the Chinese for shameful execution. Between Tatar and Borjigin was feud from now on, and the memory of the cruelty of the Chinese paymasters of the Tatars remained constant also with the Borjigin, who were as proud as they were troublesome and poor. Kabul was the great-grandfather of Chingis-Khan, through his second son.

The father of Temujin-Chingis was Yesugei-Bagatur, Yesugei the brave, and Yesugei was such another as Kabul Khan, or any of the rough squires of the steppe. The Chinese chronicles dub him a leader of ten, a 'corporal,' the measure of their contempt for these petty nobles of the steppe. In fact Yesugei was a poor enough man and though he won for himself the leadership of a small confederation of clans and tribes he was not a great figure even judged by the nomad scale. He was no king, as Rashid the Persian historian claims, but only another adventurer, a bagatur, who had left his own people to seek his fortunte.

Yesugei, hunting one day with his hawk in the valley of the Onon, saw a man of the forest Merkits leading home his young bride, a girl of the Olhonod tribe. They had stopped by the river, the girl standing by the horse-drawn *kibitka*, the tent on wheels, while her bridegroom had ridden a little away. Yesugei saw that she was fair and that she was of a tribe into which his own clan married. He felt the urge of his youth in him as he saw her standing there by the tumbling river, and with the blood hot in his cheeks he rode back to the camp to tell his two brothers of his sudden purpose.

Arming themselves, they rode swiftly to the river, where the young couple were still halted. The bridegroom saw the three brothers riding towards him, arms in hand, and their purpose was clear enough to him as it was to his bride. The girl, who was called Hoelun, spoke urgently to her lover.

'There is nought good in the look of these three. They will certainly kill thee, so quickly fly. If thou shouldst save thy life may it befall thee to have a wife like me. So thou shalt remember me, call her by my name.' So saying she took off her shift and give it him for remembrance, and he, taking it, his dark eyes blood-shot and burning, struck his horse and was gone over the edge of the valley. The brothers pursued him, but he escaped them.

Returning, they took the woman, Yesugei mounting the horse that drew the *kibitka*. As they went she wept for her young husband.

'My husband! The wind has not ruffled the hairs of thy head. Thy belly has never known hunger. But now that thou hast fled, what hard days will be thine.' The sound of her cries stirred the waters of the Onon and the leaves of the forest along the valley.

Yesugei's brother, riding by her side, cut short the lament. 'Thy husband has already fled over many a hill-crest, crossed many rivers. Though thou shouldst weep, he will not turn his head. Seek his traces, thou shalt not find them. Stop thy cries then and cease to weep.'

So they brought her home and gave her to Yesugei to cool his hot young blood and bear him strong sons.

The father of Temujin was not rich enough to pay the mating price for his bride, nor hot enough blooded to fight alone for her, nor did he have other followers then save his own brothers. As he grew older he won followers, they had their own vassals, *bogon*, and they made their raids and forays, chiefly against the Tatars, winning slaves and women for themselves, making allies where they could. The greatest of these allies was Togrul, Khan of the Keraits, who became *anda*, or sworn brother, to Yesugei.

Hoelun was not pregnant by her first husband and Yesugei knew beyond all doubt that his first-born was the son of his own loins. He was born the day his father came back from a foray against the Tatars, bringing with him one of their chiefs as captive. To mark the occasion the captive's name of Temujin was given to the new-born son. Three other sons she bore him later, and one daughter. By a second wife he also had two sons.

Yesugei felt himself a man of power and substance. His eldest born must be fittingly betrothed. When the boy was nine years old the father took him out to ride with him to the tents of the Olhonod, his mother's people, so that they should find there a maiden to whom he could be pledged. He led with him a remount horse as a betrothal gift.

As they rode over the broken country they met a certain cunning old lord called Dai Sechen, who cried out to Yesugei: 'Brother-in-law, whither ridest thou?' Yesugei answered: 'I am riding to the uncles on the mother's side of this son of mine, to the clan of Olhonod, to ask for a maiden.' And the wise old man told him flatteringly: 'Shining eyes and a bright face has thy son. Yesternight I dreamed that a hawk, bearing the sun and the moon in his claws, had lighted on my wrist. I said to my fellows: "Sun and moon we see only with our eyes, but now a white hawk bearing sun and moon has lighted on my wrist. Verily, this is a good omen!" Now, brother-in-law, at this very time thou art come with thy son and thou hast solved my dream. Truly, it spells fortune for thee. Our house has never quarrelled with others over lands or vassals. We have always had fair daughters whom we have offered to your lordly house and you have made them queens and wives of kings. When a match is made it is meet the groom should have substance and the bride beauty. Brother-in-law Yesugei, at home I have a daughter, still of tender years. Ride with me and you shall see her!'

The wise old man had recognized that Yesugei's son was a good match and his flattering tongue brought them to his tent. What the boy Temujin thought as he rode with the two grown men we cannot know. His bright boy's eyes probably watched the wide sky for the flight of cranes, or scanned the steppe for the swift movement of a hare, delighting in the space and the air, thinking the old man's words strange and beyond his understanding. Little but woe and bitterness was to come to him from this wooing and the man who was to be the proudest in the world would know the worst humiliation from that girl who was waiting in the tent, as little understanding as himself what all this honouring of guests meant, or who was the strange boy.

Yesugei saw the girl was good enough to look upon, and hastened to finish the affair. They made their agreement and the father left his son behind, according to the ancient custom, with the family of her bethrothed. A relic, this, of the mother-right which was the first form of social organization they had known, many centuries ago, in the time of their ancestors, the children of the brown wolf and the grey doe who had mated on the mountain whence sprang the river Onon.

'My son is afraid of dogs. Don't let dogs frighten him,' were Yesugei's last words as he left the future lord of the world to the care of his betrothed's family. He rode off and was never to see his son again.

On the way home he came across a camp of Tatars who were feasting some occasion. Yesugei felt hungry and thirsty, nor was it polite, according to the nomad custom, not to join in any meal with those one encountered on the way, so he got down from his horse and halted there to refresh himself. They knew him at once for their ancient enemy and though the law of the steppe forced them to give him hospitality they treacherously mixed poison with his meat and drink.

Three days later the stricken man found his way back to his own people, dying, almost blind. 'There is pain in my heart. Who is near me?' he asked. Munlik, son of his old retainer Charakh, came forward and the dying man bade him care for his children so young and so weak, and to bring home Temujin.

Munlik rode to fetch the boy home, but they came back too late. Yesugei was already dead, troubled in heart at the fate of his children left with no protector. He had good cause to be troubled. His rule had always been an uneasy one and his followers took the first chance to rid themselves of Hoelun and her children. The widow was refused admission to the sacrifices and when she protested the women told her to leave their camp and pastures. She was expelled with her family from the clan.

It was spring. They were moving by stages towards their summer pasture when the followers of Yesugei deserted her. The old man Charakh tried to hold them back, but they repulsed him roughly, wounding him in the shoulder. The boy Temujin came to him in his tent and wept, part from sorrow at their hurt to his only friend, part from fear. The widow Hoelun now showed herself for the fearless woman she was.

Taking the horse-tail banner she mounted and rode after the deserters. By right she was now head and leader of them all and they must come to her bidding. The brave woman shamed a few of them into returning for a while, but one by one they slipped away again, to rejoin the strong confederation of the Taijiuts. 'The deep water has dried up, the bright stone has broken in pieces,' they said.

The four brothers, the two half-brothers, the sister, the mother and an old serving-woman were all that was left of the *ulus* of Yesugei. They lived by the river, on the fringe of the forest region, hunting the marmots and prairie mice, fishing and trapping game at times driven by want to feeding on roots and forest plants. Temujin, the oldest, was not the strongest, and between him and his half-brother Bektor there was bitter hatred. Bektor and Belgutei would seize the fish and game which Temujin considered belonged to him by right and Temujin and his brother Kasar complained to their mother, but she would not interfere, merely reminding them that their first duty was to avenge the desertion of their followers on the haughty Taijut chiefs. They did not listen, but flung aside the reed screen at the entrance to the tent and went out to wreak their anger on Bektor.

What they did was savage and cowardly beyond belief. Armed with bows they sought the unarmed Bektor who was herding their few horses and approaching him from front and back shot him through and through. The helpless boy met his end bravely, only calling on them not to desert his brother Belgutei.

Like a prophetess of old, their mother raged at them as they came back from the bloody deed. 'Save your shadows, you have no companions. Save your horse's tail, you have no whip. The wrong done by the two Taijiut chiefs is unbearable. When you should be thinking of avenging yourselves on your foes, you do this thing,' she concluded bitterly.

These foes were not idle. His father's kinsmen, Targutai-Kiriltuk and Todoyan-Girte, the two Taijiut chiefs, knew that so long as Temujin lived they had an enemy and that in the uncertain life of the steppe it were better to be rid of him for good. So they raided the widow's little camp, calling out that they meant no harm to any soul but only wanted the boy Temujin. He had fled to the forest, and there he hid till hunger drove him out, to fall straight into their hands.

Targutai caused a wooden Chinese stocks to be locked around his neck and sent him to spend a night in every camp of the Taijiut. One night they made a feast on the banks of the Onon, leaving only a weak youth to guard their prisoner. Temujin struck him with the edge of the stocks, stunning him, and escaped to the river, hiding in the reeds with the water up to his nostrils.

They searched for him high and low, and a certain Sorgan-Shira, a serving-man in whose tent he had been treated kindly, saw him and told him to be careful.

'It is for cunning like this the Taijiut hate thee. Have a care and I will warn thee when it is safe.' The search was called off and Sorgan told him all was clear. But Temujin knew he could never get home in the heavy stocks and in the night he made his way to Sorgan's friendly tent, which he discovered by the sound of the churning of the *kumys*, for this was the duty which the serving-man and his family performed for the great Taijiut lords. Sorgan and his two sons welcomed him kindly, hid him under a cart-load of wool and, as soon as all danger was past, gave him a young unfoaled mare, a skin of *kumys* and lamb's meat for the road, and a bow and arrows for protection.

They lived their poor nomad life, while the boys grew strong and hardy, gaining courage and skill with the years. Kasar was already winning fame as an archer and Temujin was known as a wise and crafty youth, of no small courage if challenged. Complete ruin almost overtook them when thieves stole their eight grey geldings, leaving only one horse on which Belgutei was then luckily away hunting. Temujin, as soon as Belgutei was back, took the horse and pursued the thieves. Tracking horse-thieves needs skill and patience, but Temujin got unexpected help from a youth who had seen the horses driven by. Bogurchi was the name of this ally, who gave him a fresh white horse, and rode with him for three days till the tracks led them to a pasture where they saw their eight grey geldings. They drove them off, hotly pursued by the horse-thieves. One thief, on a white horse, drove ahead of the rest and began to shoot at them from his bow. Temujin halted and shot back, then darkness came on and the pursuit was dropped.

The two lads were in fettle at their exploit and swore eternal friendship. Temujin had won his first vassal, and one who was to serve him faithfully to his death. He was man enough now to defend his own and to win friends to his side. Nor was this all that these adventures on the wide steppe gave him. The man who could track horse-thieves for many days learned also the art of moving swiftly, of knowing the ground which concealed his enemies, and of striking hard at the decisive moment. The conqueror forgot nothing and learned much in this hard youth of his.

It was time for the next stage in his life. He remembered the days he had spent in the tent of Dai-noyon, the wise, and the maiden Bortei, to whom he was betrothed. It was time to wed and claim his own in this direction also. The old man Dai welcomed him kindly and the maiden was given to him to wife. As soon as he returned to his own tents Temujin sent for his sworn companion, his vassal Bogurchi, and the latter, athirst for the life of the steppe, did not even wait to bid his father farewell, but took his black sheepskin and mounted his old yellow horse.

He had now a friend, a wife, and a sable coat, for this wedding-gift Bortei had brought to her mother-in-law, the grim old Hoelun. He had four lusty brothers and his horses and sheep. The boy was a man and in his ears his mother's words of vengeance were a never-ceasing music. She had a lot to forget, this woman who had borne sons to the stranger who raped her from her own first husband, this woman who had known only the brief glory of a freebooter's wife and then the bitterness of widowhood and poverty. Let this bright-eyed, cunning Temujin win her back something of all she had lost.

He was afraid of her, the bitter woman and the wise counsellor, the widow who had the courage of a man and the decision of a warrior. She had been shamed as a girl and humiliated as a woman. She would now find comfort as a mother. She was first in honour among all of them in their wandering life, and the girl Bortei who now shared her son's bed did not take her place. Bortei indeed could have felt no great joy in her new life under the old woman's dominance in this poor camp, the memory of her own home where life was more settled and the folk richer, still fresh with her. She too was of strong character and a hot temper, though she dared not show it in these first weeks among the Borjigin. Her school was to be Hoelun's school, the hard one of the nomad woman, but her destiny was to be greater and her humiliation even deeper.

2. The Heroes' Oath

THE youth who married Bortei was no ordinary one. The character of the conqueror was already formed and, meagre though our sources are, we can still form some idea of it. The strongest influence in his life must have been his passionate, ambitious mother, for ever reminding him of his father's prowess, of the need to avenge himself on the Taijiut chiefs who had taken away his men, of how he must win followers for himself like a true *noyon*, a prince, and fight for overlordship on the steppe. He was resourceful, careful and brave, able to suffer hardship, cruel and treacherous among men whose very life forced them to cruelty and treachery. He was a very determined youth and a very bitter enemy.

The old Mongol clan had long ceased to be an organization based on blood relationship. Men of noble blood created new clans, new tribes of many different families, with their own vassals, serving-men, slaves and men-at-arms. The steppe was full of such overbearing lords, each as petty, fierce and quarrelsome as his neighbour. Even the great Togrul, Khan of the Keraits, was no more than such a lord, glad enough to take help from even a half-successful adventurer like Yesugei, Temujin's father.

From time to time groups of these adventurers banded together to make one of their number 'Khan' in order to give them greater security in war, better organization in the chase. But they considered him only as the first among equals, in no way as a king or ruler. Every youth of noble family and ability might aspire to such position and Temujin was looked on as a promising young man who would no doubt also play his part when the time came. A vague urge for unity was there among the clan leaders, and the need for it was pressing. This young feudal society could give no security, no safety or law, until someone bound all these unruly chieftains together. The grave Moslem merchants from Samarkand or Bokhara, the wealthy Uighurs from south of the Altai mountains, coming through with their caravans on the northern road to China, were no less disturbed. They would welcome the appearance of a strong figure who could impose order on all this turbulence, build a nation out of these quarrelling chiefs and beggarly nomads, thereby making the great ways safe for the caravans.

Temujin himself knew all the clan feuds and the personalities of the different leaders, was clear in his own mind who was the best ally, who the most dangerous foe. He could not read or write, but he was not ignorant. As a child he had passed a short time in the tents of his wife's people,[1] nearer to the Great Wall, had, maybe, seen towns and chaffering in the markets and was well aware that life was not all the hard struggle and bare existence that had so far been his.

In seeking for a friend the first person to whom Temujin naturally turned was Togrul, Khan of the Keraits, his father's old sworn brother. Togrul was a little richer than his neighbours, his tents were pitched nearer to civilization, Chinese subsidies found a ready way into his pockets.

'In the old days,' said Temujin, 'Togrul was my father's friend, and so to me also he is like a father. He is dwelling now on the banks of the Tula, in the blue pine forest. I will give him this black sable coat my wife has brought.'

When Togrul accepted the coat he could not conceal his pleasure. 'I will gather up for thee the folk who split away from thee and join them to thee. This will I remember ever in my heart.'

It was all the young man had to give, the first sign of prosperity in his life, this sable dowry brought by his wife, but never was gift bestowed to better advantage. The rumour of it spread through the steppe and a few days later an old man, one of Yesugei's former vassals, rode in from the hills with his son. 'I give you my son Jelmi. Let him saddle your horse and open your door.' The knight had got his first squire.

After the first success was the first and worst defeat, for nothing was to come easily to this man.

There is always a deathly stillness in the early half-light before dawn and the old serving-woman of Hoelun was roused by the trembling of the earth from the hooves of galloping horses.

'Mother, mother,' she called to her mistress, 'rouse speedily.

[1] There is some evidence that part of his childhood was also passed with Togrul, his father's friend, among the Kerait and that he here first met Jamuga. See p. 58.

The Taijiut brothers, our old fearful foes are surely upon us!'

'Awaken the children,' said Hoelun. Temujin and his brothers were on horse in a moment, their two followers with them. He took his mother on his own remount horse, but for Bortei, the young wife, there was no horse and she was abandoned in the panic flight. The old servant put her in a *kibitka*, harnessed to a spotted cow, and they trundled away along the little river Tungel. The raiders were not from the Taijiut, but those forest Merkit from whom Yesugei, years before, had stolen Hoelun.

They had their revenge this day, for the axle of the cart broke and the raiders speedily came up. They had already seized Yesugei's second wife, the mother of Belgutei, and the old serving-woman's pretence that she was on her way to shear sheep in a rich man's tents could not deceive them. They opened the door of the *kibitka*, saw the young and beautiful woman inside and knew they had taken the girl-wife of Temujin.

They pursued him to the mountain of Burkan, where he hid in the deep forest. They had his wife and could take their revenge for the old hurt of the rape of Hoelun, so they left him there and went their way with the two captive women.

The cautious fugitives hid for three days and then decided they were safe. It was not of his lost wife Temujin had been thinking in the interval, but of his own preservation. He turned to the sun, hung his belt about his neck, his cap upon his wrist and, striking himself on the breast, bowed down nine times and poured out a libation of mare's milk. 'The mountain Burkan has saved my poor life. Henceforth I will make sacrifice here and call on my children and grandchildren to do likewise.' So he made submission to the eternal Blue Sky.

To this day the great national games of Mongolia, *nadom* as they are called, are held each year in memory of this escape of Temujin. That wise young man, having preserved his slender force, now set to work to get back his wife. The Merkit had given her contemptuously to the athlete Chilger, younger brother of the man from whom Hoelun had been stolen. The Mongol chronicle tells us that Temujin went now to the Kerait Khan to remind him of his friendship, and also to Jamuga Sechen, Jamuga the wise, Temujin's own *anda*, or sworn brother, to seek aid against the Merkit. It was given they say, and the Merkit camp stormed at night, Temujin desperately calling out the name of his wife as he raced through the black tents in the light of the moon.

But the truth was probably not so romantic, if we believe the Persian Rashid. The Kerait Khan got Bortei back by diplomacy and she returned home nine months later to be delivered of a son, Juchi, 'the unexpected,' in her husband's tent. A hard blow to the young man's pride, for his eldest son to be sprung from another's loins and his wife sent back to him like a discarded slave. A hard blow for the young wife also to be abandoned for the mother who lorded it so haughtily in the tents of Temujin. She bore him three more sons and many daughters, saw other women taken to wife by this conqueror, and always kept the place of honour, yet between them there was no longer any respect. Later, she fooled him publicly with the camp minstrel.

Belgutei's mother, given to some slave or serving-man, could not survive the shame, and disappeared into the forest, never to be seen again.

Jamuga, Togrul and Temujin certainly made a campaign against the Merkit, destroying their raiding party and seizing their women, but Temujin can only have played a subordinate part. However, he here renewed a boyhood friendship with Jamuga and the two swore to be eternal friends.

'The old men say that when two make themselves *anda*, then they both have one life. One does not leave the other and they guard each other's life. Such is the law of this common tender friendship. Now we will again cement our friendship and love one another more strongly.' They then exchanged gifts and made a feast by a cliff, beneath the thick trees, and at night they slept under one blanket.

The two were fast friends for a year and a half, young men of great gifts among the nomads. Jamuga was wise and crafty, his clan were herders of sheep, and he no doubt had engaged in much traffic with those who live in towns. He was a restless, ambitious youth, a lover of new things, a man always ready to take advantage of division in the tribes. Temujin was no less ambitious. His blood was prouder than that of his friend, and his people were horsemen and lordly herders of horses. Hoelun filled him with her endless tales of the past glories of his house. Old followers of Yesugei drifted in to the camp, and their talk was the same. Bortei also had a shame to avenge. If her husband became great among his people, much might be forgotten. The two jealous women had no love for the young Jamuga, who shared their lord's blanket at night after the feast.

Around these two young men, adventurous and resourceful, many families and fragments of clans had begun to gather. It was only a matter of time, sworn friendship or no, before a split should come between them. During the summer migration they quarrelled over the pasture, Jamuga wishing to keep his sheep in the river valley, while the horse-herds wished to drive further on to the grassy slopes of the hills.

Temujin, troubled, told Hoelun of the dispute and asked her advice. Before she had time to speak, Bortei had burst out: 'Men say of Jamuga *anda* that he loves the new and despises the old. Now he has tired of us. Do his words not harbour some evil thought against us? We must not halt but press on into the night. Better to break for good and all with him.' 'Bortei says well,' her husband answered and they rode on into the night.

Many things were decided in that night. The fate of the world was in that dark ring of rumbling *kibitkas*, driven by the troubled women. Inside the circle were the cattle, goats and their few sheep. Outside rode the shadowy horsemen urging on the anxious, huddled herd of remount ponies and milch mares. The rumour of the break with Jamuga had sped before them and the steppe was heavy with anxiety in the deep night. The Jaijiut, camping near, heard the sound of hooves, the cries of the animals and the rumble of the carts as this embryo of a nation hurried towards the uplands. The sounds in the uneasy night boded no good to them and they hastily struck camp, marching also through the night to join Jamuga. The instinct of Temujin's hereditary enemies told them that the decisive moment had come and that henceforth all who hated or feared Temujin must be with Jamuga.

Temujin halted in the first light, and as the sun came up over the hills he saw one after the other horsemen hastening up from the river valley to join him. Many had been the anxious family councils in the night as to which of these two lords, the former sworn friends, was to be the leader of the Mongol tribes. The new-comers were of many clans and tribes, some of them even from Jamuga's own people. Temujin had achieved his first ambition and won back the position his father had held. He was now the leader of his own *ulus* with the right to claim that he was the first among the Mongol lords.

The round black tents were pitched all about him, the women busy at their tasks, the brightly coloured herds of horses moving in the distance across the slopes of the hills, the herdsmen with their long-noosed poles riding slowly round their flanks, their eyes alert for thieves or raiders. Now it was Temujin's work to show himself indeed a lord and to strike princely bargains with these greedy chieftains.

One of Jamuga's clan came to him with flattering words, explaining his desertion Mongol fashion by an elaborate dream full of allegorical animals and allusions to Temujin's divine mission. The cunning words finished, he came to the point. 'If thou shouldst make thyself a lordly king, then with what wilt thou rejoice me?' Temujin answered: 'Should I become such an one, then will I make thee ruler over ten thousand.' The cunning man was not satisfied. 'I have told much of great import. If thou givest me but ten thousand, what joy is this? If thou givest the rule over ten thousand, then let me also choose thirty lovely girls for wife and do thou also whatever I ask of thee.'

The bargains were struck, the promises made, and the chiefs and leaders met together in the *kuriltai*, or tribal council, there deciding to proclaim Temujin Khan and give him the title of Chingis. The meaning of the title is not known. The Chinese translate it 'Son of Heaven' and 'Perfect Warrior,' though it may be derived from a Mongol word meaning 'strong,' or, more likely still, have some mystic, shamanistic, religious meaning. The band of adventurers gathered around him after their decision was made and swore their heroic oath to this new leader and lord of the steppe.

'If thou wilt be our ruler we will fight for thee in the forefront of every battle against countless enemies; should we win fair women and lovely girls or goodly steeds as booty, we will yield them to thee. In the chase we will outstrip all others and hand over to thee the game we take. Should we break thy command in battle, or harm thy affairs in peace, take from us our wives and goods and leave us in the desert wastes.'

Chingis busied himself with the organization of his followers. It is not likely that as yet he invented a great deal that was new in his first organization, but in such a rude society, formed on such an unstable basis, it was sufficiently complex and evidence of rare energy and talent in the young Khan. Four were appointed to be his own guard, armed with bow and arrows. Three were given charge of the food and drink of the new confederation. One was set over the *kibitkas*, to be the camp commandant, another was to overlook the slaves and serving-folk, while four, including his brother Kasar, became sword-bearers of his own guard. Two were to train the horses, three to watch over the herds, one to care for the sheep, while four had the important work of being the messengers of the Khan.

Subodai, the brave, the greatest of his cavalry leaders, was already among his followers, a youth barely in his 'teens but full of a chivalrous devotion to his lord and burning to distinguish himself in the coming battles. 'I will gather for thee like an old mouse, fly for thee like a jackdaw, cover thee like a horse-blanket and protect thee like a felt in the lee of the wind. So will I be towards thee,' he told Chingis. For the latter had already discovered the secret of success among rulers of men, to combine unbounded love for himself with generous gifts, cunning flattery and merciless hatred towards any who fail or desert.

As soon as his position as Khan was confirmed Chingis sent messengers to Togrul of the Keraits, his powerful friend and neighbour, to tell him of the fact. 'It is very good,' Togrul said, 'that you have chosen Chingis your Khan, for how could you Mongols do without a Khan? Do not undo what you have agreed in council.'

It has been argued that Togrul showed a foolish benevolence towards this new and ambitious ruler, but in fact there was nothing unnatural in his attitude. Since the death of his friend Yesugei, the Mongols had been without a leader and the powerful families had either fought one another, to the general discomfort, or wandered from this leader to that, as unstable as the Gobi dust. Now they had a leader and would have all the advantages coming from their new unity. He himself was no greater chief than Chingis or Jamuga, and it would never have entered his head to imagine himself a great monarch threatened by a young and ambitious rival. Such a picture of the politics of the steppe, common though it is among most biographers of Chingis, is a false one, coloured by our own ideas of kings and kingdoms. Poor Togrul was not to imagine that a few years later his fame was to spread to Europe as the mythical Prester John, the great Christian monarch of the East.

Indeed Chingis himself was no king yet. In their oath the heroes swore to obey him in war but in peace merely to refrain from 'harming his affairs.' Many years were yet to pass before all this was changed and he had accomplished his revolution among the Mongol peoples, years in which he was still to suffer much, and more than once to be within a hair's-breadth of ruin and destruction.

Two messengers also bore the news of the election to Jamuga, who did not receive it so quietly as Togrul. 'Why did his friends turn Temujin, my *anda*, against me with their words?' he asked bitterly. 'Why did you not proclaim him Khan when we were together and what is your aim in so proclaiming him now? Strive to keep the heart of Temujin *anda* at peace and serve him loyally.' The last words were the traditional advice of a feudal lord to vassals, but the bitter questions show that Jamuga was angry and suspicious at the break. They show also that it was no sudden decision, that intriguers had been for long at work and that the quarrel over the pastures and Bortei's warning were only the pretext for what had already been planned in secret.

Temujin had won his first friends, and he had made his first and bitterest enemy. No man ever raised up more persistent foes against himself, but of them all none was to exceed Jamuga in his hatred and the dark unyielding violence of his enmity. The story of their hatred is an heroic epic in itself, coloured as it is with the constant memory of that broken friendship, of the time when they slept covered by the same blanket, under the lamp-like stars, that seem so close in the clear still nights of those eastern plains and forests. But something deeper even than this was in the opposition of these two men, something it is hard to disentangle from the Mongol saga or the Persian chronicle. For Jamuga had also a vision of Mongol unity, a different one from Temujin's, of what kind we cannot clearly know, though as the story moves on we get glimpses of it through the wild and bloody passion of their feud.

3. War and Hate

'GIFTED with wisdom, capacity and cunning,' says the historian Rashid of Jamuga, but 'a great intriguer.' 'He loves the new and despises the old,' the aristocratic Bortei had said of him, as she urged her husband to break with his sworn friend. He was certainly opposed to the proud herders of horses and was the champion of the shepherds, a hater of the turbulent aristocrats. Yet it would be too much to say that this man was the leader of the oppressed against the rise of the new feudal monarchy, that he was in any sense a 'democrat,' as so great an authority as Professor Barthold would have us believe.

Certainly the growth of the new aristocracy and the final collapse of the old blood clans must have meant a great increase in poverty among the nomads. The gradual concentration of property into the hands of the nobles, whether they were of the old Mongol lineage or the leaders of vassal clans, *bogod*, could only mean that the number of those who had no horses or cattle of their own must rapidly grow. Particularly the poorer nobles were affected by this. Rashid tells us that Jebei, afterwards to share with Subodai the glory of some of the greatest Mongol victories, was such an impoverished noble, a member of the Taijiut tribe, the old foes of the Borjigin. 'The reason why Jebei quit the Taijiut and came to Chingis-Khan was that the Taijiut tribe became weak and Jebei wandered alone over the mountains and hills. When he saw that nought could come of this, in weakness and despair he came to the service of Chingis-Khan and became his liege.'

Jamuga may have felt for the weaker members of the Mongol tribes, for the crowds of beggarly nobles and the vassals whom no one could feed, but it must be remembered that he himself was a noble, that his policy was always based on building up a rival group to that of Chingis, and that he never spoke or acted other than as a feudal lord himself. Nor indeed could he. Restless spirit, as keenly aware as Chingis of the plight of his people (perhaps they had talked of it together, at night, as they rested beneath the horse-blanket), he could for all his feeling of injustice, his vague sympathies, act in no other way. For neither his mind nor any other man's could at that time and in these circumstances conceive of a different society. He hated the aristocrats, as his actions showed, but he was one himself and he could not do without them. The first duty of the lord was to feed and clothe his slaves. His rancour against his old friend grew and it spread to all his followers. His own younger brother, wandering with his herds in the hilly pastures, came upon a follower of Chingis guarding a troop of horses. Jamuga's brother drove them off in the hours just before darkness. The herdsman pursued him and coming up with the robber in the night shot him dead with a truly aimed arrow.

Jamuga, bitter at his brother's death, called together his men and rode over the hills to settle accounts with Chingis. In this first clash he was victorious, and drove Chingis to take shelter in the valley of the Onon. Riding home from the fight he seized seventy nobles, followers of Chingis, and took a frightful revenge for the injuries he had suffered, boiling them alive. The fame of this dreadful deed roused those who were still hesitating as to which of the two leaders they should join. Chingis had been defeated in battle, but Jamuga was the enemy of noble blood. One after another they rode into the camp of the former and swore themselves his men.

Among those who came in to Chingis now was that same Munlik to whom the dying Yesugei had once entrusted him. Munlik had ridden off then with the rest, deaf to the frantic commands of the widow Hoelun. He came back now, a middle-aged man, the father of seven sons, one of them Kokchu, a famous sorcerer and shamanist. Munlik married the woman he had left to her fate years before, but in this third marriage also Hoelun was fated to find great sorrow, so that even her age she was not to spend in quiet and forgetfulness.

Chingis was now approaching maturity, but he was still only a petty chieftain of the steppes, no greater man than his father. At the feast he ordered after Jamuga had drawn off his men, the women quarrelled bitterly over questions of precedence, while the drunken nobles proved no less fiery. One of them stole a bridle and wounded his half-brother Belgutei so that the Khan himself had to restore rude order among them with a wooden club. Yet he did keep order, and this was the feature which the peoples of the steppe found most important. Among the other tribes there was none and the steady drift to his banner continued.

'The Taijiut *beks* (chieftains) disturb us in vain and alarm us,' said one group, deciding to give their allegiance to Chingis. 'But this lord Temujin will doff the coat he wears and give it away. He is a man who has a country, feeds his warriors and keeps his *ulus* in good order.'

The opportunity soon came for a safe campaign which would 'feed' the warriors with what they loved best—the booty of a defeated enemy. The Chinese had been having trouble with the Tatars and a general with a punitive force advanced into their territory. The Chinese had an excellent knowledge of all the tribal feuds and had no difficulty in persuading Chingis, through his old friend the Kerait Togrul, to march with them against his hereditary enemies. The Tatars were beaten, rewards distributed, Togrul given the Chinese title of Wang, or prince, and Chingis a minor military title meaning, by one of history's little ironies, 'commander of the frontier.'

Togrul, now the Wang-Khan, was not popular among the steppe peoples. He had come to power by the murder of his own brothers and was a narrow, weak, ambitious man. But he had great possessions and a high-sounding Chinese title; with the lord of the Naimans he held the strongest position among the tribes. For Chingis it was of the greatest advantage to have him on his side at this moment, for his enemy Jamuga was actively planning his destruction.

In 1201 a gathering of tribal leaders on the Kerulen proclaimed Jamuga Gur-Khan, lord of the people, and so made an open challenge to Chingis. There was something in the nature of a conspiracy in this act, for we read in the Chinese official history that an oath was taken: ' "Whoso betrays our plans, may he be broken like the banks of this river, and cut off like these trees," and so saying they stamped down the banks, and felled the trees with their axes.' The struggle for leadership in the unification of the Mongols and 'all those who dwell in felt tents' was entering a new phase. The Wang-Khan and Chingis gathered their forces to meet the new menace, but though Jamuga was defeated the battle was not decisive.

In following a clan of the Taijiut during this campaign Chingis himself was shot in the neck. The day had been a hard one and both forces rested in their places on the field of battle. Chingis lay in great pain, the blood clotted around the arrow wound. Jelmei, his faithful squire, was by him and tenderly sucked the wound clean. A terrible thirst tormented the stricken leader, that awful, inhuman thirst of the wounded on the battlefield. Jelmei, covering the wounded man with his clothes, crept naked into the Taijiut camp, seized a bowl of curds, and came back with it to his lord. Mixing it with water he gave it to him to drink. Three times the enfeebled man drank and the the darkness fell from his eyes and he took heart. As he sat up, the light began to show in the eastern sky and he saw that he was in the midst of a pool of blood.

'What is this?' he asked. 'Could we not have gone farther away from here?'

Jelmei answered: 'In my haste I did not think to move, and indeed I was afraid to leave you. So I sucked your wound and swallowed your blood and my belly has taken no small measure of it.'

Then Chingis, aware of what had happened, said in astonishment: 'When I was in such wise, how didst thou dare to go naked into the enemy's camp? Had they seized thee, then thou wouldst have said that I lay here wounded.'

'Had they seized me,' Jelmei answered, 'I would have said that I was minded to desert to them and that you, learning this, tore off my clothes and while you prepared to slay me I got away and fled to them. They would have taken my word, clothed me and made use of me, and I, leaping on one of their horses, would have come straight here.'

Chingis said: 'When the Merkit surrounded me on the Hill of Burkan, thou didst defend my life. To-day thou hast sucked my wound and, at risk of thy life, found curds for me and given me to drink, restoring my spirit. These three services I will never forget.'

The next war was once more against the Tatars, and this time was a struggle to the death. No male life was to be spared, save children no taller than the axle of a cart. The Tatars sold their lives dearly but they could not hold out against the strongly-disciplined force which Chingis had gradually organized from among his turbulent followers. From the Tatars he took his second wife, the maiden Yesugen. He was now approaching his middle years, when a man wearies of the flesh of the first woman he has taken to wife, and seeks to find again his vanished youth in the fresh beauty of a girl. Bortei, the mother of his sons, was still the first and honoured wife, but Temujin passed his nights now in another tent.

Yesugen, perhaps sick and frightened of the ardour of this middle-aged warrior, perhaps humbly wishing to please this conqueror who had humbled her people and slain those nearest to her, said to him: 'I have an elder sister, called Yesui, who is also a beauty. She is worthy to be a Khan's wife. She has but just married and I know not where she is.' Or perhaps she wanted this elder sister by her to be a comfort in the enemy's camp.

Chingis answered: 'If she be really beautiful, then I will command her to be sought out. But when she is found, wilt thou be willing to yield her thy place, since she is the elder?' Said Yesugen: 'Let me but see her, and I will yield her my place.'

Then he sent his men to seek Yesui and they found her in the forest where she was hiding with her young husband after the defeat of the Tatars. The young man fled and they brought her to Chingis. One day a little later the lord was sitting outside his tent with his two young wives, drinking *kumys*, when he heard a deep sigh from Yesui. His quick suspicion aroused, he had them search the camp for strangers, and in a few moments the young man who had been her husband was brought before him. 'Thou art the seed of my enemies and come hither to spy. I have slain them all and thou art of no more account,' and he cut off the youth's head himself, before the eyes of Yesüi.

There was something merciless and fierce in Chingis that was different from the ordinary cruelty of the nomad life. Perhaps it was the memory of his early humiliations, above all of the seizure of Bortei by his enemies the Merkit, and the contemptuous way in which they had soiled her before sending her back to his camp. His own followers felt the richest joy in life to be in the chase. Not so with Chingis. 'The pleasure and joy of man,' he told his followers, lies in treading down the rebel and conquering the enemy, in tearing him up by the root, in taking from him all that he has, in making his servants wail so that the tears flow from eyes and nose, in riding pleasantly upon his well-fed geldings, in making one's bed a litter upon the belly and the navel of his wives, in loving their rosy cheeks, in kissing and sucking their scarlet lips.'

This was the mind of a man who was to unite his people and organize them into a nation, who was to lead them to the conquest of the rotten empires of Asia. His life made him so, the tasks he set himself demanded such qualities. In all his career one can feel for him the same mingled disgust and admiration one feels for the founders of the great capitalist enterprises of the last century, men who also stopped at nothing, ruined their enemies gleefully and stole their wives and daughters no less gleefully, men who organized great empires also, empires of steel and power and publicly always preached caution, moderation and sobriety.

The time was fast approaching when the lordship of the forest and steppe must be decided once for all. The great khans could no longer tolerate one another's rivalry and even the Wang-Khan was beginning to look with suspicion upon his old friend Chingis. The two of them were warring to the westward now, against the forest Merkits and the powerful, more civilized Naiman. Wang-Khan defeated the Merkit, seizing their women and making slaves and vassals of the men. But the Mongol chronicle is careful to note that he gave none of his booty to Chingis. The two of then joined forces to march against the Naiman, and when they came up with the enemy, Wang-Khan deserted the Mongols in the night, leaving his camp-fires burning in order to deceive them. Jamuga, the bitter enemy, saw his chance and came at once to the Wang-Khan to whisper evil against Chingis. The latter was intriguing with the Naiman, he insinuated. 'You and I are like the snowbird,' he said to the Wang-Khan, 'but your ally is like the wild goose. Come cold, come heat, the snowbird is true to the north; but when the winter comes on, the wild goose flies off to the south.' And that weak, ambitious man, so proud of his foreign title, listened readily to the cunning words.

A man of a clan friendly disposed to Chingis heard Jamuga and remonstrated angrily with him. 'Why dost thou use wiles and slander against thy good brother?' he asked him. Jamuga, a man who saw more deeply than his fellows, might have answered that where there is a broken friendship between men of strong will and opposing dreams of life, there will be hatred so strong that it can know no bounds.

In any case, the Wang-Khan must soon regret his rash step, for a sudden raid of the Naiman on the tents of his elder son Sen-Kung carried off men and women and threw the Kerait ruler into a panic. He sent a hasty messenger to Chingis. 'Send me thy four knights,' he begged, the first intimation we have that Chingis had now a properly-organized army under his command, the beginning of that mighty weapon that was to win him the world. They saved the life of Sen-Kung and brought back the captured men and women.

A gleam of wisdom seems to have come to the old Khan at this moment. The man who commanded these heroes must surely be the supreme ruler one day. Togrul's own brothers and sons were weak.

He would adopt Chingis so that their two peoples might be united and strong. So they made between them a pact of father and son. 'In war we will fight together against the enemy. In the chase we will hunt together. Should any men make trouble between us we will neither hear nor believe them, but will on all occasions speak direct with one another.'

Chingis, so that the alliance might be fully confirmed, asked that Sen-Kung's sister be given in marriage to his eldest son Juchi, who was now of the age when he must be found a wife. He suggested that his own daughter should also marry Sen-Kung's son. All Sen-Kung's pride was revolted at this. Chingis was an upstart adventurer, moreover all men knew the story of Juchi's doubtful birth. 'Should a maid of our house go to theirs, she will be but a servant wench to stand at the door. Should a maid of theirs come to us she will sit with us like a mistress.' The proposal was rejected, for the old man did not have the strength to resist his son. 'And the heart of Chingis grew cold.'

The watchful Jamuga heard at once of this coldness and he speeded to profit by it. In that rude society news spread like wildfire. He sought out Sen-Kung and told him the old lie that Temujin was intriguing with the Naiman. Some of Chingis's own relations, jealous of his power, had left him for Jamuga, and joined in the evil work. They urged Sen-Kung to destroy Chingis completely. 'For thee we will slay all the children of mother Hoelun,' they said, and 'I will go to the very heights, or down to the farthest depths,' so each of the traitors promised, persuading him.

Sen-Kung sent word of their proposals to the Wang-Khan his father, but the old man would not listen to such treachery. 'Heaven would cease to love us and protect us. Jamuga's words are false and not to be trusted.' Sen-Kung pleaded long with the old man, pointing out that the nation gathered together with such difficulty by his father and grandfather would fall a prey to Chingis after Togrul's death if something were not done. The old man continued to refuse and then, wearied, washed his hands of the affair.

So the tribal council, the *kuriltai*, was summoned, and a plan was devised for seizing Temujin by treachery. A shepherd, a domestic slave, bringing in mare's milk from the pasture, overheard the plot and told it to a comrade. They decided to ride away secretly to warn Temujin, thereby winning freedom and a rich reward.

Forewarned in time, Temujin drew up his men to prepare for this, the greatest battle of his life so far, while the Wang-Khan, Jamuga at his side, was also sorely troubled as to what should be the outcome of his clash with his adopted 'son's' warriors. So they went into battle, Jamuga, the sworn brother, Wang-Khan the 'father,' against Chingis-Khan and his knights and men-at-arms. The struggle was a bitter one, decisive for neither side. Seng-Kung was wounded by an arrow, but Chingis, when night fell, deemed it prudent to withdraw.

When day dawned he drew up his men to call the roll and his heart contracted as he saw that three of the bravest and best were missing, Ugedei, Boro-Kula and Bogurchi. 'Ugedei, Boro-Kula and Bogurchi, truest of my men, together lived and together died, not desirous of parting.' They continued the retreat, not daring to sleep at night, but all the time awaiting the enemy's attack. In the early light Chingis saw a horseman riding wearily towards them. It was Bogurchi. He struck his breast, called out to the sky, as Bogurchi told him of his escape. 'My horse was killed under me. As I went on foot I saw the Keraits draw off around the fallen Sen-Kung and seized the chance to take a baggage-horse.'

Hardly had he finished than they saw another horse appear, two legs dangling down each side. It was Ugedei and Boro-Kula, riding together on one horse, Boro-Kula's mouth smeared with blood where he had sucked an arrow-wound in his comrade's neck. Chingis, weeping with joy and relief, tended his wounded battle-friend himself, burning the wound with fire and giving him medicine to quench his thirst. The little army, less than 3,000 men, continued to retreat slowly down the Khalka river, provisioning themselves with the game they were able to kill, till they reached the Buir lake region. Here they halted on the bank of the little river Tungel where the grass was lush and the horses were able to eat themselves into condition again. From here Chingis sent two messengers to the Wang-Kahn to tell him in the poetic, rhythmical speech used by these men who knew no writing, that he wished for peace.

'O Khan my father,' ran Temujin's message, 'when your uncle . . . for having killed your brothers . . . drove you to take refuge, did not my father come to your rescue? Did you not then become *anda* with my father, and was not this the reason I styled you father?

'When you were driven away by the Naiman, and when your brother was attacked by the Merkit, did I not attack and defeat them? Here is a second reason for your gratitude.

'When in your distress you came to me with your body peering through with tatters, like the sun through clouds, and, worn out with hunger, you moved languidly like a dying flame, did I not fall on the tribes who molested you? You came to me haggard. In a fortnight you were stout and well-favoured again. Here is a third service we have done you.

'When you defeated the Merkit, you gave me none of the booty, yet shortly after, when you were hard pressed by the Naiman, who had taken the women and folk of Sen-Kung, a full half of thy following, I sent my four knights who brought back the women, the cattle and all the folk carried off from Sen-Kung. Then also did you thank me. Why now do you reproach me?

'Do you not remember, O Khan, my father, how on the river Kara, near the mount Burkan, we swore that if a snake glided between us and envenomed our words, we would not listen to it until we had received some explanation. Yet you suddenly left me without asking me to explain.

'O Khan, my father, why suspect me of ambition? I have not said: "My part is too small, I want a greater," or "it is a bad one, I want a better." When one wheel of a cart breaks, and the ox tries to drag it, it only hurts its neck. If then we detach the ox, and leave the wagon, thieves will come and steal the load. If we do not unyoke it, the ox will die of hunger. Am I not one wheel of thy chariot?'

The message closed with a request that Mukuli's black gelding with its embroidered and plated saddle and bridle, lost on the day of the battle, should be returned and that messengers be sent to treat for peace.

To Jamuga he said: 'Out of envy and hatred you have parted the Khan my father from me. When we were boys it used to be that whichever of us two woke first in the morning, drank mare's milk in the dark cup at my father's. I was always first, and so you hated me. Now drink the dark cup at my father's to your heart's content!' To each of the treacherous kinsmen also he sent a message, half threat, half cajolery.

Sen-Kung, when he heard the messages, was full of rage. 'When did he call my father "father," or myself "friend." He called my father old murderer and me by an evil name. I have guessed the secret sense of his words—it is battle. Raise the great banner and fatten the geldings on the pastures. There is no more any doubt.'

When the messenger brought back the reply Chingis moved with his men to the salt marshes around lake Baljun. Here passed the

Uzbek merchant Hassan, from Turkestan, driving a thousand sheep and a white camel, to trade in sable and squirrel furs with the people dwelling by the river Ergun. Watering his sheep in the lake he met Chingis, was deeply impressed by him and no doubt told the news to the other merchants of this nomad genius who he had met in the refuge at lake Baljun.

Chingis was now again at a low ebb in his fortunes. The little band by the lake were literally drinking the bitter waters of affliction in those unhealthy marshes, hard put to it to keep body and soul together. Only a desperate throw could extricate them. Violent with anger and hatred Chingis sought the only way left, to prevail over his enemies by treachery. Betrayal and trickery had been used againt him. He would answer with the same weapons and strike back so mercilessly that men would tremble at his name.

4. The Kingdom of the Tents

THE message which Chingis had sent to the Wang-Khan, for all its picturesque phrasing, was a very serious diplomatic note. It was a strict reminder of his own rights and behind the conciliatory language was, as Sen-Kung discerned, a threat of war to the death if peace were not made. In such circumstances no peace could be lasting, as both sides knew, so the renewal of hostilities meant that one side or the other must perish.

Chingis's brother Kasar had left his wife and three children in the Wang-Khan's camp. He now, at Chingis-Khan's suggestion, sent a treacherous message that he had sought Chingis and been unable to find him or even trace of him in any place. So he pleaded for the Wang-Khan to treat with him through a trusted agent for his desertion.

Thus the old Kerait's suspicions were lulled. His enemy had vanished, his enemy's brother was suing for surrender. He set up the great golden tent of festival and arranged a feast for his followers. No precautions were taken against attack and not the slightest warning was received of the Mongol advance. The Keraits, taken by surprise, fought fiercely and only after three days of hard fighting was the victory secured. Wang-Khan fled towards his old enemies, the Naiman, was taken by some of their vassals and beheaded on the spot. His son went south towards Tibet, where he too was seized and slain by enemies. The Kerait were divided up among the followers of Chingis and the two daughters of Wang-Khan's brother fell to the conqueror. The elder he kept for himself, the younger he gave to his son Tuli for wife. She afterwards became the mother of the great Kubilai, Mongol emperor of China. One man escaped from the general ruin, and that was the implacable Jamuga. He found refuge with the Naiman, rousing that important people to a sense of danger which now threatened them.

Jamuga had so far tried to build up his alliances against Chingis from among the nomad steppe peoples. Now he sought to draw together the semi-settled nations, those who dwelled part of the year in towns, knew writing and had a developed trade with the great countries of Central Asia or with China. The Naiman were such a people. They had inherited the old Uighur towns and with them much of the Uighur culture. Buddhism and Christianity were widespread among them, though the old shamanist sorcerers still kept their influence. In an earlier battle they had tried to use magic to drive the wind and rain in the faces of the combined forces of Kerait and Mongol, but the elements had refused to serve them that time. The Naiman welcomed Jamuga and listened readily to his warnings.

So also did the forest-dwelling Merkit, the old enemies of Chingis, they who had stolen his young wife Bortei from him. They were not town-dwellers, but they were active traders, for the grain merchants from the Yenesi passed through their country, and they also did a great commerce in hawks and falcons. Another people, the Ongut, dwelled near the Great Wall, a peaceful, semi-pastoral folk, with small towns of their own where they traded with the Chinese. They had no wish to be disturbed and rejected all proposals to join a league against Chingis.

The latter realized that to fight the Naiman was a greater task than any he had yet undertaken. If they were to be beaten it would only be by superior skill and organization. The army was completely re-organized, the office of *Jerbi*, or quarter-master, created, and the guard, that nucleus of a permanent army which had been slowly growing up, was increased in numbers and its duties clearly defined. A council of war was held at which warning of the Naiman intentions was given by a friendly chief. 'Unless you accept peace, the Naiman will take away your bows and arrows.' 'Our horses are thin and not in condition,' was the feeling of some on hearing these words. 'How can we keep quiet when we listen to such talk,' another of Chingis's nobles cried out indignantly. Belgutei, not noted as a rule for his wisdom, spoke next. 'Should they disarm us living men, what use is that to us? Brave lads die arms in hand. Is not that glorious? The Naiman have dared to utter high words, relying on their wide lands and many people. It is no difficult thing for us, at this favourable moment, to disarm them. If we attack them, they will leave their numerous herds of horses, quit their dwelling-places and with all their people fly to the hills and forests. And so let us to horse!'

Chingis-Khan approved his bold council and, after a great hunt to supply themselves, they moved west to take up a position for their attack on the Naiman, Jebei and Kubilai leading the van. The Naiman, capturing a scout, were in high glee when they saw the poor condition of his horse. But the Mongols succeeded by a clever ruse in destroying the enemies' confidence. As their line of patrols advanced into the Naiman country they lit so many fires at night that the feeling of an enormous host advancing on them from all sides gripped the Naiman pickets. Panic reached even their Khan, Tayan, an old man who was already prepared in his own heart for defeat and death.

Tayan's son Kuchluk and the old foe Jamuga alone were undisturbed, but they were powerless to stop the spread of the panic. 'The life and body of mortal man are doomed to suffering. It is all the same. Have it your own way and let us march to meet our enemies,' Tayan answered his son's reproaches of cowardice.

His army retreated into the hills, hard pressed all the time by the Mongol patrols. Tayan, watching from afar, asked Jamuga, 'Who are these that drive our men like wolves pursuing a flock of sheep to their pen?' Jamuga answered: 'They are the four hounds of my Temujin, fed on human flesh. He holds them on an iron chain. These hounds have skulls of brass, their teeth are hewn from rock, their tongues are shaped like awls, their hearts are of iron. In place of horse-whips they carry curved swords. They drink the dew and ride upon the wind. In battle they feed on human flesh. Now they are unleashed from the chain. Their spittle runs, they are full of joy. These four hounds are Jebei, Kubilai, Jelmi and Subodai.'

Tayan then drew his men back to the next height, but the enemy still came on. 'Who is that behind, like a hungry kite straining forward?' he asked again.

'That is Temujin, my *anda*,' said Jamuga. 'He is clad from head to foot in iron armour and he has flown here like a hungry kite. Do you see him? Once you said that let the Mongol only appear and like the lamb not even his hooves and hide will remain. Now see!'

Jamuga had given up the struggle. As the Mongols advanced he realized that no force could withstand them, that all his efforts had been for nothing. He might scare the timid Tayan, sow panic among the Naiman, but he knew well enough that his own song was sung, whatever happened now. The Naiman made little resistance, Tayan was killed, his son Kuchluk fled to join forces with the Merkit, and Jamuga with a few followers made off into the steppe to lead an uneasy life of brigandage.

The Merkit were defeated next. Their chief Toktoa was killed, while Kuchluk fled to Turkestan, to the empire of the Kara-Khitans, there to organize a last resistance against the inevitable doom that was on his tracks, for Chingis had learned the lesson that he must never leave an enemy undestroyed.

Chingis took his fourth wife, Kulan, from the Merkit, so completing his revenge for the rape of Bortei. She was a beauty whose fame has come down in Mongol poetry and she was his companion afterwards in many of his campaigns. The whole of the peoples of Mongolia from the Great Wall to the Altai Mountains, were now, with unimportant exceptions, his subjects and he had made a kingdom such as had not been known there since the last of the Turkish Khans had died.

Jamuga was seized by his followers and given up to the victorious Mongol. Chingis, with a gesture typicial of him, slew the traitors who were thus false to their master and offered peace and forgetfulness to his old friend and enemy. Jamuga answered him with a tragic resignation that is full of nobility, the kind of noble clarity that a man sometimes attains when he sees his life all spent behind him and no future to give him hope or vision.

'In those days long ago, when we became *anda*, we cooked our food and ate together, we spoke words to one another that cannot be forgotten. Then there came people between us who set us against one another. Remembering those old words, I grow red with shame and have not the courage to face my *anda*. Thou dost wish me to become thy comrade, but though I bore the name, in fact I should not be so.

'To-day thou hast gathered peoples under thy rule and there is no way I can be thy comrade. If thou dost not slay me I shall always be like a louse on your collar or a spine on your inner gate. Because of me thou wilt be uneasy by day and at night sleep fearfully. Thy mother has wisdom: thyself art a hero: thy brothers have talent: thy comrades are valiant knights: thou hast seventy-three geldings in thy great lords. But I from childhood have had neither parents nor brothers: my wife is a babbler: my comrades not trusty. So my *anda*, above whom is the sky, has surpassed me. Now grant that I may die quickly that my *anda's* heart may be at peace, and that I may die without shedding of blood. Then I, after death, will be for ever the protector and helper of thy descendants.'

When Temujin was told these words he answered sadly.

'Jamuga *anda* went ever his own way. He is a man who might be corrected but he desires no more to live. So be it.' Jamuga was then crushed to death, without the shedding of blood, so that his spirit might dwell unchanged among men, for it was the Mongol belief that man's spirit resides in the blood.

Jamuga was dead. Among the Mongols no man now dared make an open opposition. The army moved back to the head-waters of the Onon, to the valleys where Temujin had spent his desperate youth, and there the banner with the nine white horse-tails was raised and the council of the nobles called together to proclaim him Khan of all the peoples dwelling in felt tents. The year was 1206 and he was in his fiftieth year. The Mongol name, for so long fallen into obscurity, from being the name of a small tribe had become that of a mighty nation. Those other great nations who dwelled in their walled cities on either side of this new kingdom were still blissfully unaware of the revolution which had taken place among the despised nomads. How great in fact that revolution was, what far-reaching changes Chingis had made in the course of his fight for power, we shall now see, and see at the same time how and why they impelled this unknown adventurer to lead his horsemen to the storm of the whole world as it was known to him.

5. The Forest of Many Trees

THE *kuriltai* on the Onon is one of the great events of world history. Here the nomad adventurer was proclaimed king and his monarchy organized, while there gathered about him the leaders of all the tribes and peoples of Mongolia whom he had united by his genius and military skill. He now had by his side not only brave generals but wise counsellors also, men who wrote down his decisions and saw to the execution of his judgments. The chancellor of the Naiman Khan was a Uighur called Tatatungo. After his master's death he was taken by Chingis into his own service where he performed great and important work in spreading the Uighur culture in the Mongol court.

When first taken prisoner and brought before Chingis he had with him his golden seal. 'What use is this seal?' Chingis asked him. 'Every time my lord wished to levy silver or grain or give a commission to any of his subjects, he caused his orders to be obeyed by this seal, in order to give them an authentic character,' the Uighur told him. From that day Chingis commanded that all his orders be marked with a seal which he entrusted to Tatatungo. It is not too much to assume that in the great work accomplished at the *kuriltai*, the advice and experience of this first minister played its part. By now also Hassan, the merchant of Turkistan, and the Christian Mongol merchant Chinkai, both of whom had 'drunk the waters of Baljun lake' with Chingis and his band of heroes after their defeat by the Wang-Khan and Jamuga, were in his permanent service. They were men who knew well other lands and the ways of the great rulers of the settled nations to west and east.

We have called Chingis, King, and king he now was in fact, but it must be remembered, if we are to understand his achievement properly, that he was the first king among the Mongols, who till this time had never known the institution of monarchy. When he had been proclaimed Khan many years before, after the break with

Jamuga, it was no royal power that was then invested in him, only the leadership of a little band of adventurers. Yet the need for such a centralized power as he now held, for a firm feudal state such as he now created, had been long felt among the Mongols and the germs of all its institutions had been in existence even in the days of his father Yesugei. Chingis created nothing new. He only understood with truly remarkable insight the meaning of the changes taking place among his people, speeded up those changes through his own impetuous energy and genius, and gave them final form.

As the old blood clan broke up, as separate houses fell away and formed their own clans with their vassals and serfs, seeking to find in this way a firm basis for their individual nomad economy, away from the hampering ties of the old patriarchal union, new forms of social organization and new relationships grew up out of the old. These nomad seigneurs, *noyod*,[1] to use the Mongol word, were wealthy horse- and cattle-ranchers who were compelled to lead an independent existence with their herdsmen and shepherds.

For protection they must keep their own armed force. So to the great lords there came youths of other noble houses, in search of adventure and a livelihood, to take a pledge of chivalrous service as *nöküd*,[2] 'companions' or esquires. The *nökür* brought with him nothing but his horse and his arms. The lord, the *noyon*, must keep him, and the better the lord is able to keep his followers, the more free and generous towards them he is, the greater will be his reputation, his knightly fame.

So the same institutions developed among the Mongols as in feudal Europe. The poorer, weaker and more unfortunate lords sought the protection of the stronger or the wealthier and a gradual process of unification went on. A group of such adventurers would elect a Khan to lead them in battle or the chase, thus winning greater security for their property, the opportunity to increase it at the expense of enemies and to maintain their followers and vassals in fitting state. Yet this very striving for security and unity inevitably, in the conditions of nomad life, led to greater insecurity and anarchy. The old society had been destroyed, the new had not grown up. Life was a series of wild forays, of continual desertions, of the splitting up of groupings and tribes, a constant struggle between the Khans.

Temujin was made Khan of a small group who broke away from

[1] Singular is *noyon*.

[2] Singular is *nokur*.

Jamuga's leadership. None of the existing Khans joined him, and even the most important chiefs of his own clan of the Borjigin viewed his rise with mistrust and took the first chance of betraying him to the Wang-Khan of the Kerait. Hence the merciless character of this steppe warfare. Everything called for one man to unite the Mongol people and the nobles themselves were conscious of the need for unity. But when every wealthy owner of great herds, every ambitious Khan, saw himself as the potential leader of the people, the man who in fact was to unite them could only succeed through the physical destruction of his rivals.

Rashid ed-Din tells us of a clever and shrewd old man of the Bayaut tribe who summed up this situation perfectly and enumerated those Khans who aimed at the overlordship of the steppe and imperial greatness.

' "Sacha-beki," he said, "of the tribe of Kyiut-Yurkin, has the desire of lordship, but he is not fitted for it. Jamuga Sechen, who is for ever setting one against another and contriving tricks and pretences to work his own way, will also fail to achieve it. Juchi-bera, that is Juchi-Kasar, brother of Chingis-Khan likewise nurses such a desire and seeks to distinguish himself by his strength, power, skill and his shooting from the bow. However, he also will not succeed. Neither will Olan-Udur, of the tribe of the Merkit, achieve it. But this Temujin, that is Chingis-Khan, is of such a kind, quality and aptness for this, for lording and for ruling, that he will verily reach the King's dwelling." These words he spoke in rhyme and artfully.' Rashid is careful to emphasize that the old man spoke these words 'at the time when Chingis-Khan had not yet made himself *padishah* (supreme ruler) and there was a lust for the first place and lordship among the tribes.'

Of the greatest importance in this new feudal society was the institution of *nöküd*, the esquires of these khans and nobles, who formed a kind of chivalry of free companions and were the nucleus of the military state organization which was growing up. The *nökür* might be a member of the Khan's guard, or an officer in command of a tribal levy, or a great general. The important thing was that his allegiance was a personal one to his lord and was quite independent of any ties of family or clan. He might be a messenger or ambassador, an organizer of the chase and a camp commander, or simply a personal attendant on the lord. He was a free man, without the obligations of the vassals or the degrading toil of the slave.

The lord in turn must feed and clothe his men, find them arms, booty and women. Temujin well understood that it was by winning a reputation for lordly and chivalrous treatment of his followers that he would win the boldest fighters and most devoted servants to his banner. He liked to be thought 'a lord who feeds his slaves and possesses men-at-arms'; to have men say of him, 'this prince Temujin will doff the coat he wears and give it away; get down from the horse he is riding and give it away. He is a man with a country who feeds his warriors and keeps his *ulus* in good order.'

Mongol society was exceedingly poor, its productive power very small. In the early days of Temujin's warfare, the capture of a few silver ornaments was a great event. A saddle or bridle was a piece of property of very great value and every new mouth to feed and lusty warrior to provide for was an economic problem to be solved. Naturally enough it was solved in war. Every clan leader became a danger and menace to his neighbours, while the growth of this military aristocracy and their chivalrous following, the *nöküd*, could only mean the final break up of the old clan and the enslavement of the poor and weak. So long as the blood tie lasted the poor had some hope from the obligations of the clan to all its members. In this new society they had none. Instead of being maintained, they must now maintain. 'Those who were adept and brave fellows I have made military commanders. Those who were quick and nimble I have made herders of horses. Those who were not adept I have given a small whip and sent to be shepherds,' Chingis declares in the 'Sayings' reported by Rashid.

The organization of these esquires into a military bodyguard was the next step. Chingis was not alone in this, for we read of the Wang-Khan also possessing a guard. But it is this step which is the most important one in the revolution then taking place, for from this guard the military leaders are chosen and soon in place of the old blood chief we have the feudal military leader appointed by his lord to rule a domain (the Mongol *ulus* or grouping of tribes) and give him faithful allegiance in return.

Chingis had the genius to see what a tremendous weapon the institution of the *nöküd* could be if developed and properly used. In place of the unruly Khan, the treacherous aristocrat of the old clan leadership, he proposed to substitute his own vassals, bound to him by inviolable allegiance, at the head of the subdued, defeated and broken tribes. From the day he first became Khan, when he was still an unknown adventurer, he paid special care and attention to his personal following. This following strengthened and developed in the struggles which ensued and from among them he made the most talented into the little group of picked military leaders, devoted to himself, which later won him such fame, 'the four Knights of Temujin,' his 'four hounds.'

The great *kuriltai* of 1206 gave final form to the organization of the Mongol feudal state. To each of his trusty leaders Chingis now gave his own domain, or *ulus*, made up of different tribes or fragments of tribes, dwelling in a definite piece of territory and pasturing their stock there. The leaders now became *noyons*, princes, and each had the obligation of providing from among his subjects so many men for the army of their Khan, this man ten thousand, that one a thousand, even down to a hundred men. This was the tribal levy. But in addition he had developed the guard into a splendidly disciplined regular army to which each free family must send recruits. The officers of the guard were chosen from among the faithful who had drunk with him the bitter waters of Lake Baljun, in the days of his defeat. The privileges of the guard were great, but the discipline in turn was strict. No such military force existed anywhere in the world at that time and such a closely-knit, highly-trained and courageous body of men had rarely taken the field.

Each seigneur, or *noyon*, was given possession of suitable lands to maintain his people. He had the right to the first choice of the spoils of the chase, then after him the lesser nobles and free men shared in order. The serfs and slaves could keep nothing for themselves of the game killed or captured and the first privilege given to a freed slave was 'to take for himself the game and beasts trapped or killed in the chase.' Military booty was divided in the same way, a portion being set aside also for the Khan. Even the serf, however, might own stock, for without horses and cattle no Mongol could live. But they and their families had to perform many services for the lords, killing goats and sheep for him on certain great occasions, sending their cows and milch mares to pasture with those of their lords for certain periods and also paying actual tribute each year in cattle. There were many of these Mongol simple folk who were unable to perform even these services, so poor were they. They were called 'houseless folk' and when Chingis organized his army at the great *kuriltai*, a special corps was formed from among them and a shepherd given its command.

All those who had served him well now received their reward. Faith and loyalty had not been in vain and were paid for at the most generous rates by the conqueror. It was time to codify the changes that had been made, to give the seal of law to all that had been done. So might the lords of ten thousand and a thousand know more clearly their rights and their duties, while the task of ruling this great multitude of poor and turbulent horsemen would thus become easier.

On the basis of the ancient customs of his people he drew up a code of law, the *yasak*. Chingis was an innovator, more than any man he had destroyed the old life of his nation, yet he was careful to take from its past all that might strengthen and fortify the empire he had built up. We have no complete knowledge of his *yasak*. The best account is the work of an Egyptian historian, Maqrizi. It contains the law on sexual relations, punishing fornication and sodomy. It prohibits untruth, magic, spying and interference with one another's conduct, quarrelling or participation in the quarrels of others. Clearly this last is an effort to stamp out the petty clan feuds which had so long made secure life impossible among the nomads. It is interesting to note that 'whoever receives merchandise and goes bankrupt thrice is put to death after the third bankruptcy.' We do not know when this was introduced into the *yasak*, but it could not have been long before the settled conditions of the new empire allowed a considerable growth of trade.

A number of laws are simply rules of desert hygiene and codifications of the hospitality of the steppe or of its religious prejudices (for example, the punishment of death for any who piss upon water or ashes). Then follows a code of behaviour for the army and the rules with regard to slaves and prisoners. If a soldier in the heat of battle drops his bow or quiver the trooper behind must pick it up. Failure to do so means death. It is interesting to find the frugal nomads compelled to wear their clothes without washing until they should be worn out, a necessity forced on them by the hardship of their life.

The rules for the inspection of troops and arms are most strictly laid down. The Khan must carry this out in person, must know everything the soldiers should have with them and punish a soldier who lacks any article of equipment. The women accompanying the armies must do all the work and undertake all feudal services imposed on the men while the latter are away fighting. On their return from a campaign the soldiers must perform certain services for the

Khan. It is important to find the *yasak* confirming by law the position of the new class of feudal nobles, the *noyod*, and dividing them into commanders of a thousand, a hundred and ten.

If a noble committed a fault and the Khan sent even the least of his servants to punish him, the guilty noble must throw himself down on the earth before him in humble submission till the royal representative had inflicted the chastisement to which he was condemned, though it were death. The Khan desired all nobles to address themselves solely and directly to himself and pronounced penalty of death against all who addressed themselves to other than the Khan, a very important provision indeed.

His adopted brother he made chief judge, with instructions that all his judgments were to be inscribed on tablets, while his son Jagatai was to see to it that the *yasak* was enforced throughout the empire. That it was enforced with implacable severity wherever the Mongols ruled we know from many sources and it proved an invaluable weapon to them in binding their empire together, though it was an intolerable burden for the conquered peoples, as well as for the poorer Mongols themselves. It was the fullest expression of the Mongol feudal spirit, with all the harsh intolerance that distinguishes every purely military civilization. The Japanese are perhaps the only nation in the world who are an exception to the law that militarism and a high culture cannot exist together.

The Mongol army was to prove itself in the next fifty years the most powerful military weapon ever forged. For this the credit must go to Chingis-Khan, its creator. The social changes which he had so accelerated among his people had also their effect on military tactics. His first army was made up of clan levies, each clan forming its own division in battle, with its own clan and tribal leaders. By 1206 this system had completely disappeared. The clans themselves were so broken and dispersed that they were no longer blood unions but the feudal appanages of military leaders directly under the Khan's command. In addition the guard formed a regular army of great mobility, shock power and disciplined strength. In war the Mongols were able to adopt the tactics of shock attacks by deep and extremely mobile formations which never failed to shatter the thinner and ill-disciplined ranks of their enemy, even when the latter's numbers were greatly superior.

Because he was a military commander, with trusted lieutenants and a disciplined force behind him, Chingis could take swift decisions and strike lightning blows which were impossible to his enemies, hampered by family divisions and jealousies. The campaign against the Naiman is a most striking example of this, where the small Mongol army, on its worn-out horses, by a series of swift marches over a great extent of country struck terror and surprise into a superior enemy who was better equipped and resting on his own bases.

Chingis himself, now fifty years old, was a man of indomitable will, violent energy and great mental power. These qualities were born in him, but they had been developed to their highest point by the conditions of his long and bloody struggle for power. Power was his passion and this passion happened to coincide with the path of development and the interest of his people. He had the confused and misty sensualism of all men of violent will and a vague religious mysticism of his own. The historian Juzjani tells us that as he drew on in years he would fall into long epileptic trances and it was in these trances that he spoke the words which were taken down by his awed followers—the 'Sayings' of Chingis-Khan—and given the force of law.

Yet he showed his great mental power in the strength with which he dominated his own stormy nature, the prudence which he employed in all things. Towards an enemy he showed no mercy, but to a follower who made a mistake he could be lenient and even generous. Like all his people, who lived such a hard and insecure life, he loved to gorge himself and drink to stupidity when occasion permitted a feast, yet he was careful to be neither a drunkard nor a glutton. When he received a present of six flasks of Chinese wine from a friendly chief he declared that 'a little of this stuff raises the spirits, but an overdose confuses them' and in general he refrained from an overdose.

He was superstitious, himself practising magic and divination by burning the shoulder-blades of sheep in his camp-fire till they cracked, but he was perfectly aware that superstition is also an excellent weapon for fooling the ignorant and we know at least one occasion when he used it thus deliberately. He had few prejudices and it was no doubt his great mental energy which made him such an eager listener to those with better education and wider experience than himself. Few conquerors in history have made better use of their intelligence service than this illiterate nomad.

When the work of the great *kuriltai* was over, when the organization of his empire was completed and he was once more on the march, an emotion very like love overcame him as he looked down upon his hosts camped in the green valleys of the Altai. 'My archers and warriors are dark like a vast forest of many trees,' he said. 'It is my care and intention to sweeten their mouths with the gift of sweet sugar, to bedeck them in front, behind and upon the shoulders with brocaded garments, to seat them upon goodly geldings, to give them to drink from pure and tasty rivers, to vouchsafe their four-legged beasts good lands with abundant grass, to order that from the roads and ways which serve the people all rubbish, roots and harmful things shall be cleared, and to allow no thorn or pricking plant to grow upon the pasture.'

Pride? Perhaps, but pride which had so grown that it already mingled with some other deeper emotion. In the strange mind of man the violent and lonely struggle with reality which is the basis of the strong will and the love of power sometimes creates new emotions, reveals new features, which hide for a moment the treachery, cruelty and dark lusts which are the other side of that struggle. These creative emotions may be the justification for life, the single parts which go to form the joy of being of which even the vilest pages in human history nevertheless form a part.

PART III

The War with China

1. The Sorcerer's Sedition

THE work of rounding off the new kingdom was quickly and efficiently accomplished. Subodai followed up the remnants of the Merkit and completed their destruction. Kubilai was dispatched after Kuchluk, the fugitive Naiman prince, and occupied the northern part of the modern Semirechiye, the region of seven rivers. Before this was done, however, events of enormous importance were to take place.

First, the Khan's eldest son Juchi by a sharp thrust into the forest and river regions of Siberia subdued the Kirghiz and the Oirat, thereby opening the road by which the grain from the rich Yenisei region might flow abundantly into Mongolia. With the grain traffic came the Moslem and Uighur merchants who controlled it, eager men of affairs and well-informed politicians. A Uighur was now chief minister to Chingis, Uighur merchants moved freely through his territories and the culture of this remarkable people was everywhere adopted by the Mongols. The *Idikut* (holy majesty) of the Uighurs, uneasy in his capital at Bishbalig, near the present town of Urumchi, because of the harsh suzerainty of the emperor of Kara-Khitai, sent ambassadors to make submission to Chingis-Khan.

The event was a notable one and Chingis showed how much he appreciated it by giving his daughter in marriage to the *Idikut*.

The Uighurs were from now on to be the dominant force in all civil and cultural affairs of the new empire. Chingis was deeply attracted by their civilization and himself owed very much to contact with this able people. Mr Lattimore is of opinion that the Uighurs are the original stock of the Turkish tribes. In any case they were the first to adopt agriculture and a settled existence. When their own empire was at its zenith in Mongolia from 750 to 850 they were in close and friendly relations with the great T'ang dynasty of China and their rule stretched down as far as the Turfan oasis.

They practised Christianity, Manichæism and Buddhism and

were the medium for a remarkable penetration of Western and Iranian influences into China. Though they had long ago lost all political influence they still remained in the twelfth century by far the most important commercial and cultural influence among the Turkish and Mongol tribes. It is not assuming too much to attribute to this Uighur influence the extraordinary tolerance shown by Chingis towards all religions as well as a goodly portion of the statesmanlike grasp of great affairs which he showed in all his dealings. Chingis had at least good reason to feel no fanatical devotion to the shamanistic spirit worship of his own people. The last attempt at any opposition to himself came soon after the *kuriltai* and came from the shamanist Kokchu, the fourth son of Munlik, whose religious name was Teb-Tengri ('Ascending to Heaven'). Munlik had seven sons, each, the Mongol chronicle tells us, 'more wicked than the other.' Teb-Tengri was a man of great influence among the tribes and there is some evidence that he played a considerable part in the election of Chingis as emperor at the *kuriltai* of 1206. Possibly he hoped to win wealth and position for himself by this. If so, he was disappointed, for another, much older man, was appointed Bek, or chief shaman, to wear white robes and ride upon a white horse.

The sons of Munlik were soon busy intriguing against the unity of the new kingdom. First they tried to embroil Chingis with his brother Kasar, the renowned warrior and archer. The seven brothers beat up the doughty Kasar in the camp and when he complained to Chingis the latter answered him in great irritation: 'Once thou didst boast that none might risk a fall with thee; how then dost thou permit them to beat thee?' Kasar wept with mortification and could find no words with which to answer. Worse was to follow. The subtle Teb-Tengri, seeing his rebuff, seized the chance to whisper to Chingis that 'A spirit has declared unto me the sacred command of the Eternal Sky. First Temujin will rule over the peoples, and then Kasar: if thou shouldst remove Kasar then the issue will be in doubt.'

Chingis sent the same night to Kasar's domain, had him seized and brought in as a prisoner. Good friends at once rode to inform Hoelun, their mother, of the dispute between the brothers. Hoelun, wasting no time, harnessed a white camel to her *kibitka* and drove through the night straight to her son's camp, arriving at dawn. Kasar, his hands bound, his cap and belt taken from him, was already standing before Chingis who was examining him on the supposed conspiracy. As his mother burst into the tent Chingis was completely taken aback and frightened by the terrible appearance of the old woman. She, as was her way, wasted no time, but untied her son, took the cap and belt from the silent and unresisting Chingis and put them back on Kasar. She sat down, her anger showing in every gesture, and with a quick twist of her old hand she undid her dress. Her shrunken breasts hung down to her knees as she bent forward, her hands cupped upon them.

'Do you see?' she asked. 'These are the breasts which you two sucked. What crime has Kasar committed that thou shouldst destroy thine own flesh? When thou wast small, with thy brothers thou didst suck this breast, but Kasar alone was able to suck both breasts and give me relief. Though the soul of Temujin has genius, Kasar has strength and cunning with his bow. Now all our enemies are at last destroyed and Kasar is no longer wanted!'

The words were bitter, but the old woman, remembering that day when the two brothers as boys had murdered their own half-brother, remembering all the dangers and hardships since, her clear mind seeing how fatal this quarrel might prove to the still young kingdom, must have felt a passionate anger against her son. Chingis could not face her look but turning away said: 'I am frightened and ashamed.' For all that, he secretly took away the greater part of Kasar's vassals, though he failed to keep the story from reaching his mother. But the bitter old woman had exhausted her strength and died, as she had lived, in sorrow and pain.

Teb-Tengri was successful. As the news of the coolness between the brothers spread men came to him from all sides to give him their allegiance, even from the vassals of Chingis's own younger brother Ochigin. Ochigin went to the seven sons of Munlik to protest in person, but they only reviled him and forced him to his knees to ask for pardon. Ochigin went straight to Chingis's tent to tell him of his humiliation. He was listened to in silence, for it seemed as though something paralysed the conqueror's will with regard to the sons of Munlik. Perhaps he recalled the part played by Teb-Tengri in investing him with the supreme power at the *kuriltai*, perhaps he was genuinely afraid of the latter's supernatural powers. Again it was his women who forced him to action.

Bortei, his wife, jumped off the bed, covering her nakedness with a blanket, tears of mortification in her eyes as she listened to Ochigin's story. 'What sort of order is this?' she cried. 'They have beaten Kasar and humiliated Ochigin. If in thy very lifetime they destroy thy brothers, majestic as cedars, then after thy death the people, like grass blown by the wind, or a flock of birds, will not submit to thy sons who will have become small and of no account.'

Chingis roused himself. 'When Teb-Tengri comes hither to-day,' he told his brother, 'do with him as thou wilt.'

Ochigin secretly arranged for three powerful wrestlers to wait outside the tent and when the sorcerer came at last into Chingis's presence, he seized him by the collar and began to wrestle with him.

The sorcerer's cap fell by the tent fire and his father, who was standing by, understood that the end had come. Sadly he picked up the cap and kissed it, as the struggling men reeled out of the tent. There the three wrestlers gripped Teb-Tengri and broke his spine. 'Teb-Tengri refused to try his strength with me and lies there without getting up. It is clear he is no ordinary fellow," said Ochigin grimly as he came back into the tent.

The dead man's six brothers came menacingly in and silently barred the exit from the tent. Chingis, alarmed, jumped up and cried to them to stand aside. Rushing out, he called his guard to surround him, had a tent pitched over the dead man, and himself struck camp. A guard was placed over the corpse, which was then secretly removed and buried in the night. On the third day Chingis caused the tent to be opened and when it was seen the sorcerer was no longer there he announced to the people: 'Teb-Tengri beat my brothers and slandered them unjustly. For this Heaven closed its heart to him and withdrew his life and his body.' So the superstitious people were made to believe that the dead man had been taken away by Heaven through the smoke-vent of the tent, and the sedition of Teb-Tengri was at an end.

The Mongols were an intensely superstitious people. The air was full of spirits, good and evil, but mostly evil. The rushing of the great winds, the weird noises that echo in empty mountain spaces, the terrible storms which shake earth and sky alike in the steppe regions of Asia, were so many vicious goblins to their imagination, against whom the strongest charms could be of no avail. Chingis gravely questioned the Chinese philosopher Ch'ang Ch'un upon the reasons for thunder and Ch'ang Ch'un himself on his journey mildly rebuked his Mongol escort for rubbing their horses' heads with blood at night for protection against the goblins of the Altai. 'Goblins flee away,' he told them, 'when they meet a good man; so it is written in the books. It is not seemly for a Taoist to entertain such thoughts.'

The murder of Teb-Tengri rid Chingis of his last internal enemy and the aristocratic chieftains who had rallied to the sorcerer hurried back to their own domains. No Mongol ever dared again to challenge Chingis-Khan, for it was clear now that Heaven itself, the Eternal Blue Sky, was working actively for him. He had achieved that very necessary moral weapon which every conqueror has sought to forge for himself, a divine authority for his work.

And conquest was an absolute necessity for the new kingdom. Some writers, M Léon Cahun and the Mongol nationalist historian Khara-Davan, for example, have considered Chingis a conscious world-conqueror, impelled by the feeling of a divine mission. This over-statement conceals the real character of the Mongol invasions. Chingis had no conscious desire to subdue the world with the healthy militarism of a new-born Mongol nationalism. He did not seek war, even with China, and least of all did he seek a conflict with the powerful Moslem empire of Khwarizmia in the west. He would have engaged willingly in peaceful trade if it had been possible, but it was not.

The new empire had to enter into relations with its neighbours, to carry on trade with them on a very large scale. The new feudal class must have the marks of their rank, fill their tents with costly ornaments, clothe their wives and concubines in silks. The army had to be equipped and Mongol society could not produce weapons on a large scale. Grain must be imported also, while China in particular needed from the Mongols the raw materials of their pastoral economy in exchange for manufactured goods.

But peaceful trade was an impossibility. China was divided between two dynasties, its internal economy was in collapse, and the northern Kin dynasty was threatened in addition by a great peasant rising, which their southern neighbours did not scruple to assist. The Tangut kingdom cut off the old Lop Nor trade route to the west and also held the caravan route into Mongolia itself, which started from Kara-Khoto, the 'dead city' excavated by Colonel Kozlov and Sir Aurel Stein. The Gurkhan of the Kara-Khitai Empire also blocked the free flow of trade between China and the West, while his pwerful neighbour, the Khwarizm-Shah Mohammed, had the ambitious aim of monopolizing the whole Western trade to China.

In these circumstances the new Mongol Empire must either fight or die. Either it enforced on its neighbours freedom of exchange or else it must itself collapse before their pressure and from inability to maintain its own social structure, with its greedy and ambitious class of feudal military leaders, on the basis of the extremely low productive power of Mongol pastoral society. Nor must we leave out of account the influence of the merchants who flocked to Mongolia from Central Asia and the border regions of the Great Wall as soon as a stable state had been created by Chingis. These merchants, Moslem Uzbeks and Buddhist or Nestorian Uighurs, were quick to see the great advantage which would come to them if a man of Temujin's genius were to establish a firm rule over Northern China. Further than this no one thought in the years immediately after the *kuriltai* of 1206. There was no dream of world empire, only the inexorable pressure of economic forces combined with the genius of one man and the cunning or wisdom of his more civilized advisers. The history of China is full of adventurers from the steppe who have won great positions, including the Imperial throne. Chingis was no ordinary adventurer and the Mongol army which he had created was in those days no ordinary instrument of conquest. The Mongol cavalry was about to commence its epic and bloody march across the civilized world, and behind that march, with all its tremendous consequences for the relations between East and West, was no fantastic destiny but the real needs of men and women, the failures and cruelties of great governments and dynasties.

2. China, the Kingdom of Drunken Rulers

OF the Tangut state of Hsi-Hsia little is known to-day. The excavations at Kara-Khoto have shown us a people with a highly-developed urban culture, deeply influenced by Buddhist religious thought and pictorial art as it developed in Central Asia from the eighth to the tenth century. Their language, written in a script somewhat resembling but totally distinct from Chinese, has only in recent years been rediscovered through the labour of Russian and French savants and the manuscripts unearthed at Kara-Khoto are only to-day being published for the first time. The Tangut state, we know from its relations with the Northern and Southern Chinese dynasties, was a powerful one and the reduction of its fortresses was to prove as difficult to Chingis as the conquest of the Kin Empire of Northern China. But of how this hardy people of Tibetan race lived we have few indications. Apparently they did not suffer as did the people of China, for Chinese governments are always complaining that the hospitable frontiers of Hsi-Hsia are a refuge for every seditious element. They appear, like the Sung, to have been in secret relations with the Red Coats, the peasant army which was in rebellion against the oppression of the Kin. But we may take it that these democratic sympathies were rather a matter of policy than of outlook. The Tangut state owed its existence to division and weakness in the mighty Chinese Empire and clearly it was to the advantage of its rulers to encourage and foment every possible intrigue and division, even when it assumed the dangerous form of a jacquerie.

China, on the other hand, was a country in full decay. Though even at this time it was still by far the greatest civilization in the world, though in science, thought and art, it was centuries ahead of any other country, China was a terrible example of the social degeneration which results from the heartless and unlimited exploitation of the people by the possessing classes. Drought and flood in the Sung period became a part of the daily life of the Chinese people.

The peasants' fields grew exhausted from the continual pressure upon them from the bureaucracy, the usurers and the army.

During the period of the Sung emperors China had to face two major foreign invasions, that of the Khitans, a Turko-Mongol people from Eastern Mongolia in the tenth and eleventh centuries, and that of the Tungusic Kin or Jurjen[1] in the twelfth. Conscription into the armies emptied the villages of their men. 'It was as though I heard the darkness choke with tears,' wrote the T'ang poet Tu Fu in one of the most desolate poems ever written by man in which he describes the visit of the recruiting officer to a deserted village. The T'ang took men to carry through their great policy of conquest. The Sung took them to defend their crumbling power against nomad invaders and the internal rebels who constantly rose up to challenge their weak and corrupt rule.

Vagabondage became so widespread that no law could check it or alleviate it, while the corruption of the officials was open and insolent as the central power grew weaker. The Russian priest Zaharov, who has written some of the most interesting studies of the condition of China on the eve of the Mongol conquest, writes as follows of the actions of the officials: 'Fear of being called to account or losing the chance of promotion inspired the officials to put children in the lists of adults capable of performing state duties and to take a money tax from them. In this way they brought the people to such a pitch that the simple folk began to murder their own children in order to avoid paying fresh taxes.' So government robbery made child-murder into one of China's social customs.

The lower officials themselves, the poorer scholars who had passed their examinations but could find no work or profitable employment, formed a great and dangerous army of discontents, ever ready to give ideas and leadership to the spontaneous movements of the desperate peasantry. In the middle of the eleventh century the great statesman Wan An-Shi tried to stop the rot and, by assisting the peasants, sought to restore the basis of Chinese economy. But the financial, political and military reforms he introduced were never properly operated and the absence of a strong central power made it impossible to check the greed of the feudal officials and generals. Wan An-Shi wished the State to become the wholesale merchant and the banker for the peasantry, destroying the baneful

[1] The Kin were the same stock as the modern Manchus.

power of the usurer and trader, but this patriarchal Utopia could never be realized in the actual conditions of Chinese life and the resistance of the merchants and upper officials doomed the reforms to an early end.

The rulers of this unhappy country took the path of every state which finds itself unable for physical reasons to carry the direct plunder of its subjects beyond certain limits, the path of inflation. The printing-press developed to such a degree in China, not from thirst for learning, but because of the need for paper money. Similarly the Sung epoch saw the growth of a great metal industry in China; iron-smelting, copper-, gold- and silver-mining, were all exploited as a State monopoly and worked by slave-labour, in order that the demand for money and more money might always be satisfied. Prices in the market at Peking on the eve of the Mongol invasion would change between morning and evening and State interference only made confusion worse.

The Sung at least had the advantage of being a native Chinese dynasty, so that their rule south of the Yangtze was tolerably firm. The Kin, however, were not so lucky. They were aliens themselves and they had to rule over two other alien peoples, the Khitans of Southern Manchuria whom they had succeeded, and the Chinese themselves. They had to bear the brunt of the frontier wars against the nomads and the constant threat of the strong Hsi-Hsia kingdom of the Tangut. When the Mongol troopers rode over the passes into the green plains of Northern China, the Kin were also engaged in a deadly struggle against the peasant league of the Red Coats, one of those innumerable secret societies which throughout their history the desperate people of China have formed to defend themselves against their oppressors. The lines of Tu Fu, 'At the palace doors the smell of meat and wine; On the road the bones of one who was frozen to death,' though they are written of an earlier and better period of Chinese history, are a vivid enough picture of the society into which the whirlwind of the Mongol cavalry broke in the year 1211.

The landless peasant, harvest failure and famine, the vagabond, the marching armies, the insecurity of commerce, the insolence of the rich families who were everywhere seizing on the best land for themselves, behaving as though 'they possessed the Emperor's power over the Empire,' these were the outward symptoms of decline. But life on the land and in the cities, at the great courts, was far from being in complete decay. Such a strong and ancient culture as the Chinese had immense powers of resistance. The cities of China, with their teeming populations, their great commerce, their busy industries, their gay tea-houses and important buildings, were as far ahead of the European cities of those days as modern New York or Chicago is ahead of an English county town. The first travellers from Europe, though they arrived in China only a few years after the devastation of the Mongol conquests, were amazed at the rich and busy life they found.

Chinese ships made great voyages from the southern ports to India. The wharves were crowded with shipping and some of the junks of those days were lofty craft indeed compared with the frail vessels which bore the trade of the Mediterranean and North Sea. Chinese industry was very highly developed, largely on the basis of slave-labour. The workshops of the great cities turned out marvels of craftsmanship and beauty for the great officials and the court, for export abroad.

Of the culture of this unhappy people, we can say that it was probably the highest ever achieved by man and that even the illiterate and half-starved peasant was a more civilized and gracious being than the feudal aristocrat of Europe in the twelfth century. This civilization had, it is true, already passed its zenith at this period. It was under the rule of the T'ang in the three hundred years between 600 and 900 that the Chinese made the greatest achievements of the human spirit. Many elements went into this culture, including even influences from Greece through the Gandhara Buddhist civilization of Northern India which spread through Central Asia into China.

The T'ang epoch was immortal for its sculpture and its poetry. The Sung painters were able to reproduce in their landscapes the lyric mystery and charm of the earlier poets, to create a pictorial poetry of nature, of man's identification with the spirit of nature, hardly less beautiful than the lyrics of men like Li Po. Chinese poetry was able to make passionate tragedy out of the love of the Emperor Hsuan Tsing for the Lady Yang Kuei-Fei; the T'ang poets were able to give us pictures of the Court ladies, of dancers and concubines, at once passionate, tender and gay. The beauty of this art is something so deep, so intimate, so fresh that it must always form one of the most precious parts of the treasure of man's soul.

Yet it would be the greatest mistake to see the loveliness of Chinese poetry and Chinese painting as things divorced from the bitter realities of Chinese life. These men who sought the beauty of mountain and lake, the swift movements of animals, the flower-like grace of women, who sang the joys of wine, the secret of drunken ecstasy, the beauties of intellectual conversation and the warmth of friendship, were fully conscious of the kind of world which gave them birth. They were for ever haunted by the evil thought of how men live in the empire of flowers, and that haunted consciousness appears in all their work.

Their strange awareness of the transience of all mortal things, of the swift current of the deep stream of time, colours everything they wrote. At their merriest and most drunken a deep sadness pervades their work. If they seek beauty and find it, it is because the vision of life around them is unbearably painful. There is nothing heroic and nothing brave in their work. When they sing of war it is with horror and disgust. If they find a refuge in the mystical contemplation of nature, if they seek to mingle themselves with the unearthly beauty of their own land, it is because it is safer and more comforting so, a refuge against the madness which might otherwise afflict them.

The Chinese poets are a mirror of the Chinese character. No other nation has ever had so many maxims extolling guile and cowardice. Before the violence and oppression of the great they are the weak man's only defence. The natural humour and gay roguery of the common man or the sensuous poet cannot find a better outlet than in sly satire, in the deception of the rich and mighty. The satire of the Chinese poets is the most devastating in all the world's literature. The little epigram by Wang Chi (A.D. 700) 'On Going to the Tavern' is not only a complete expression of the bitter humour of the Chinese, it is also what most Chinese must have thought about their country five hundred years later when it fell a prey to the Mongol invaders, so it is worth quoting in full:

'These days, continually fuddled with drink,
I fail to satisfy the appetites of the soul.
But seeing men all behaving like drunkards,
How can I alone remain sober?'

The conflicts which were shaking Chinese society to pieces found expression no less in the spheres of philosophy and religion. Confucianism in its most classic form was revived under the Sung monarchs, the faith of the bureaucrat and the stateist. Taoism, nearer to the real spirit of the Chinese people, the expression of their disillusionment in the real world and a philosophy which gives them a refuge from the battle of life, appealed particularly to the intellectual and the poorer scholar, but in the Sung period it had to yield first place to Confucianism. Buddhism with its fatalism and renunciation of life made a strong appeal to the poor and oppressed and, though the Chinese are unusually tolreant in religious matters, occasional bitter persecutions of the Buddhist priests mark this period. With the coming of the Mongols the position changed. Taoism, through the hermit Ch'ang Ch'un, early sought and obtained the special protection of Chingis-Khan, while the Mongols, who contained thousands of Buddhists in the ranks of their armies, were naturally kindly disposed towards this faith. It was Confucianism, the traditional faith of the Chinese ruling class, which had been raised to the position of a State religion by the Sung emperors, which went into decline when the old national dynasty was thrown over by the people and the Mongol rule established over all China.

For it is doubtful if even the Mongol military genius could ever have conquered China completely, re-uniting north and south, without the help of great sections of the population who were full of hatred and contempt for their degenerate and greedy rulers. That they only exchanged one yoke for another hardly less heavy, was their misfortune, and no fresh one in Chinese history, but at least the Mongols for a long period were the means of revivifying Chinese society and arresting its quick decay.

3. China Broken

THE new Mongol army won its spurs in the campaign against the Tangut. The war was successful, though it was not decisive. A rich booty in camels, bullion, silks and slaves was taken and the Tangut King gave his daughter in marriage to Chingis, but it was not till many years later that the Mongols finally broke their stubborn resistance. Events in China were one of the reasons why the Mongols drew off their forces and made a temporary peace.

The Kin Emperor had died and the new Emperor, with an astonishing lack of insight into the changes which had taken place on his frontiers, sent a mission to Chingis to demand the usual acknowledgment of overlordship. The ambassadors were rudely received, and Chingis, better informed politically than the Chinese, told them outright that their emperor was a weak fool. He fully understood the chaos reigning in China and his Moslem merchants gathered information for him as they travelled with their caravans into the great cities of the north.

He knew that the Chinese must answer his declaration of independence with war, so, like the realist he was, he prepared to strike first. His preparations were extremely thorough. In every Mongol camp the women were busy manufacturing great quantities of arrows, while the army was mobilized and special care given to the drill of the cavalry. They were made to feel that they were embarking on a national war against hereditary enemies, to take revenge for the Mongol chiefs so cruelly executed by the King sixty years before. Chingis retired for three days into his tent with a rope round his neck to fast and commune with himself, and then, going to a hill-top, took off cap and belt and made sacrifice to the Blue Sky before entering on his great enterprise.

Prisoners were brought in and strictly examined as to the condition of the enemy forces and the state of the country. Their stories confirmed the reports of the Moslem spies and Chingis felt certain that he would be successful. But he left nothing to chance. The Chinese were better equipped than his men, their generals were men of great experience in warfare, their armies vast in numbers and well-trained, their fortresses strongly held. He himself had come to power by no gentle means and a rising in his rear was not impossible. A picked force of 2,000 military police was left behind as a protection against such an attempt and to guard the pastures and tents of the Khan.

The army which finally moved out towards the passes leading over the mountains into the fertile Chinese plains was a formidable instrument of war. The heavy cavalry wore armour consisting of four overlapping plates of tanned hide which were lacquered to protect them against humidity. They were armed with lance and curved sabre. The light cavalry carried a javelin and two bows, one for shooting from horseback and another for use on foot when greater precision of aim was desired. They had three quivers with different calibre arrows, one of which was armour-piercing. The troopers carried tools, a camp-kettle, an iron ration of dried meat, a water-tight bag with a change of clothes which could also be inflated and used in crossing rivers.

All manœuvres were directed by signals and the whole army worked as smoothly as a machine. The Mongols avoided closing with the enemy till he was weakened and disorganized by superior fire and their battle tactics were arranged to allow for this. The battle formation was in five ranks, separated by wide intervals. The two front ranks were the heavy armoured cavalry and the three rear ranks the unarmoured light troops. The advance was always covered by clouds of skirmishers. As the opposing forces drew near, the rear ranks passed through the intervals and poured a hail of arrows and javelins into the enemy. When their fire had disorganized his advance they retired again through the intervals and the front ranks charged.

The Mongol invasion of China was a splendidly calculated military plan. The numerical superiority of the Chinese forces was neutralized by the superior mobility of the Mongols who pinned them to the defence of important fortified points while their own columns, in perfect co-ordination, struck out in three directions to prevent the enemy concentrating superior forces at any one point. The fortresses guarding the passes were carried by storm, and the Kin Army defeated in a terrible battle in which Chingis himself commanded the Mongol forces.

The memory of this battle remained long among the Mongols and the rumour of it spread far beyond the Chinese frontiers. Many years later Ch'ang Ch'un saw the bleached bones of the dead upon this battlefield, while the ambassadors of the Khwarizm-Shah also saw from afar the high white mound of skulls and found the ground greasy and dark with human fat. 'So men are scattered and smeared over the desert grass,' a Chinese poet wrote of an earlier war than this.

But more powerful forces than his own military genius were working for Chingis. The news of the invasion was the signal to the peasant Red Coats to rise everywhere against their oppressors, while the first Mongol victories revealed the greatest military weakness of the Chinese—the varied national composition of their armies. They included men of Mongol race who at the first opportunity deserted to the enemy, they had divisions recruited from the Turkish Khitans[1] of South Manchuria, from the Jurjens, as the Tungusic people from whom the Kin were sprung were called, and from native Chinese. In 1212 the Khitans rose against the Chinese and sent ambassadors to make submission to Chingis, while the Sung Emperor in the south, taking advantage of the difficulties of the Kin, also invaded Honan.

A cavalry raid in the winter of 1211 had captured the herds of horses of the Kin armies on their pastures north of Peking, and in the spring the rapid movements of the Mongols again brought confusion into the Chinese armies. They seem to have been absolutely bewildered by this ability of the nomads to cover immense distances with such amazing rapidity. Jebei, for example, took the important fortress guarding the mountain road from Mongolia to Peking, by a great surprise march in which every man of his corps was supplied with a remount. Surprise was always the chief weapon of the Mongols, for in almost every battle which they fought, whether in China or Central Asia, they were numerically inferior to the enemy.

As the war progressed whole units of the enemy passed over to the Mongols and were re-organized into their army. Finally in 1214, the columns united under the walls of Peking and prepared to invest the city. Probably it was hoped that the enemy would be overawed by the show of force, for the Mongols had not yet mastered the art of siege. If so, they were completely successful. The Kin minister

[1] Professor Pelliot thinks the Khitans were of Mongolian origin. If this is so their friendliness to the Mongol invaders is easily understood.

advised his Emperor to make peace. 'The Mongols have grown extremely strong. They have destroyed our bravest armies and captured our strongest fortress. If we fight them again and are defeated, then our army will no longer hold together. It is better to come to terms with the Mongol Khan that he withdraw his men and give us breathing space. Moreover it is rumoured that an epidemic has broken out among the Mongols who are not used to our climate. So give the Mongol Khan your daughter and gold and silver and silks, and see whether he will agree to peace.'

Whether or not the Mongols were weakened by disease we do not know, but Chingis gladly accepted the offer of peace, though both sides understood clearly that it could not be lasting. With an enormous booty, the daughter of a Chinese emperor, hundreds of youths and maidens as slaves, Chingis set out through the mountains for the Mongolian plateau to recruit his strength and refresh his men. The Kin princess was, by all accounts, a lady of great breeding but scant personal attractions, and the great Khan was content to give her the respect due to her position and leave it at that. It enormously increased his prestige to have this Chinese princess among his wives, though she was in fact only an adopted daughter of the Emperor and there is a suspicion of contempt in the way in which this ugly duckling of the Chinese court was given to the barbarian king. Her life, like that of most such hostages to fortune, was not to be a happy one in the rough camps and frontier towns, away from the culture and luxury which were part of her being.

Chingis sent an ambassador to the Court of the Sung, but the Kin, realizing how fatal for them an agreement between the southern court and the Mongols must prove, arrested him and turned him back. The Chinese were evidently determined on war, for they simultaneously sent an army into Manchuria against the rebellious Khitans, who were now in league with Chingis. The Emperor abandoned his capital on the outbreak of war, but his Khitan mercenaries mutinied on the march, occupied Peking and called on Chingis for help. In the summer of 1215 Peking surrendered.

This time the Mongols determined to make it clear they were no ordinary marauders. They occupied all the provinces north of the Hwang-Ho, reduced the Emperor to a petty princeling, and demanded his complete submission to Chingis. This was refused and the war went on. It must be said that these ancestors of the Manchus made a brave enough resistance and it was not till 1234, seven years after Chingis's death, that they were finally destroyed. But the Khan had humbled his proud enemy and beaten his armies; the northern provinces, as well as Manchuria and Korea, were part of the Mongol Empire, and an endless stream of captives, goods and treasure flowed through the mountain passes to the mud towns and nomad camps of the Mongolian plains and forests.

Chingis was filled with a longing for his own country, for both Turk and Mongol love the freedom of their steppes and prefer the nomad life in those great spaces, with the dry, bright air and clean winds, to the cities and sweltering plains of more cultivated countries.

> 'Tchirek River
> Lies under the Dark Mountains
> Where the sky is like the sides of a tent
> Stretched down over the Great Steppe.
>
> The sky is grey, grey:
> And the steppe wide, wide:
> Over grass that the wind has battered low
> Sheep and oxen roam.'

In 1216 Chingis was back again by the clear waters of the Kerulen, amid his horses and sheep, camping in the round felt tents in which his life had been passed. True, his nomad camp was now filled with luxuries of which he had not even dreamed as a young man. When he ate and drank, lovely girls and handsome youths made music in his tent, and his faithful followers were clothed in brocaded silk, as he had sworn they should be that day he looked down on his people encamped in the green Altai valley. He had given them sugar and delight even more than he promised. He might rest content. In China his viceroy Mukuli with the army of occupation could be trusted to finish the war with success. He himself would rule his own people and establish his position as a great monarch with his neighbours to east and west.

He had also won something more precious than rich booty and a royal wife in the war with the Kin, and that was a counsellor of great intellectual power and real nobility of character, a man who was able to make himself heard and respected in this rough soldiers' court of the Mongols. This was the Khitan prince Yeliu-Ch'uts'ai, the governor of Peking. He was a descendant of the former Khitan emperors of Northern China, whose family had taken service with the Kin when the latter drove out the Khitans. Chingis was at once deeply impressed by the tall stature, fine beard and musical voice of Yeliu Ch'uts'ai, as well as by the minister's chivalrous loyalty to his former masters. No one ever won such constant influence over him as this wise and noble man and he not only consulted him before every important decision, but also paid the greatest attention to every intervention the statesman made in his own decisions, and they were many and important.

Yeliu Ch'uts'ai had been educated from childhood by his mother, and was particularly distinguished in astronomy, geography, the calendar and arithmetic. He composed tables of the course of the planets which were in use for many centuries, and was a skilful writer and keen observer. His position was far from being an easy one in this rude military society. A certain Tangut, high in the Khan's favour for his great skill in making bows, took a dislike to the cultured courtier and went around among the Mongol nomads asking what was the use to them of a man of letters like Yeliu Ch'uts'ai. Hearing of the Tangut's efforts to turn men against him, Yeliu Ch'uts'ai answered very aptly: 'Workers skilled in making bows are necessary, but if it is a matter of governing empires, how can we do without workers who know how to manage this?' When this retort was reported to Chingis he was delighted and brought Yeliu Ch'uts'ai more closely than ever into his confidence. He knew the value of having men around him who were skilled in government and was never afraid to take advice from those with wider experience than himself.

In the quiet of the summer in the grasslands by the Kerulen he was able to consider many things and to solve the problems which had accumulated during his absence in China. They were no small ones, for old enemies had grown strong and new ones were looming on the horizon. The need for wise counsel and sure knowledge was never greater. A new crisis in his affairs had come and though he was again to prove the stronger in this fresh conflict with life, this time the price of victory was to be the pouring out of his own last effort of mind and body.

PART IV

The Road to the West

1. Kuchluk's Last Effort

WHILST Chingis was away fighting in China, great changes had been taking place in Central Asia as a result of his destruction of the nomad peoples of Western Mongolia, the Naiman and Merkit. Fragments of the defeated tribes filtered through the valleys of the Altai and across the Gobi into the empire of Kara-Khitai, a territory covering the present Chinese Sin-Kiang and East Turkestan up to the Syr Daria. This empire had been founded in 1230 by the Khitan prince Yeliu-Ta-Che, who was recognized by all the Turkish tribes as Gurkhan, or universal Khan. The capital was at Balasagun on the river Chu, and all the cities in the valleys of the Ili and the Tarim were under the rule of the new empire.

The Kara-Khitans expanded rapidly to win control of these vital Central Asian trade-routes. The Uighurs became their vassals and further west their influence made itself felt in Turkestan proper where the Emir of Samarkand and the Khwarizm-Shah both recognized the suzerainty of the Gurkhan. The Gurkhan's empire was nevertheless doomed from birth. It seemed as though it was impossible to found a stable state in those two valleys through which the Chinese overland trade must pass. To-day the very cities are only names beneath the dust, mounds of wind-corroded loess in the desert, and the river Tarim itself is no more than a dried-up water-course. Against the pressure of the nomads from the north and the Chinese and Turkish states from east and west no stable rule has ever been able to exist there. The hundred years of Uighur domination were the longest.

For all that, this area has been as great an entrepot of human culture as it has of precious merchandise. Buddhism, Manichæism, Nestorianism, the influences of India (and through India of Greece), of Iran and of Turan have all mingled there to form the marvellous art which Stein, Von le Coq and other explorers have recovered from under the sand in the last generation. Through these cities went the art and the thought of the West to mix with the native art of China and form the masterpieces of the T'ang period. Soghdian merchants and missionaries trading there brought the first letters to the Turkish peoples, the beautiful Uighur alphabet which the Mongols have retained to the present day. The Soghdians were the first missionaries of Manichæism and when the Uighurs adopted their religion, and with it their alphabet, they entered a milder and more settled life than that of the wild nomads. 'The land with barbaric customs and the smell of blood is to be changed into a land where men lived on vegetables, the land where men slew one another, to a land where they exhorted to the good,' wrote a Uighur Khan in 921, recording in Chinese the sentiments of this first and greatest of the Settled Turkish peoples. Through the Uighurs the use of paper seems to have come from China to Central Asia, to become one of the industries of Samarkand centuries before it was known in Europe.

When the defeated bands of Naiman and Merkit first appeared in the empire of Kara-Khitai in 1208–9, however, the country was in full decay. The Manichæan and Buddhist priests, robed in red, still exhorted to the good, but they both joined in bitter hatred of their Moslem fellow-citizens. The Gurkhan was himself a Buddhist and the Kara-Khitans, installed as conquerors, seem to have regarded their new empire chiefly as a source of plunder. The Moslem Turks were cruelly taxed and deprived of all commercial advantages, but so also were the Uighurs, that great commercial people. Religious differences in the empire were heightened to an unbearable degree, partly because the Khitans hoped to maintain themselves by the principle of divide and rule, partly because of commercial rivalry.

Kuchluk, the 'fortunate,' the son of the Naiman Khan, fled to the court of the Gurkhan, after his defeat by Chingis, while the sons of Toktoa, the Merkit chief, took refuge with the Uighurs. The appearance of these bands of nomads at once produced a crisis in the weakened Kara-Khitai Empire. Like all the states formed by nomad conquest, the central authority had rapidly decayed, the military leaders had seized lands for themselves and the tax-collectors squeezed the conquered people to the last possible degree in order to maintain the court and the feudal nobles.

A movement had already begun in 1207 among the Moslems against their infidel rulers, a movement of which the Khwarizm-Shah and the Emir of Samarkand took full advantage in the following year, throwing off their nominal allegiance to the Gurkhan and declaring their independence. The Uighurs also seem to have seized the chance created by the appearance of the nomads and risen against their oppressors. In 1209 the Gurkhan's representative in Uighuria was killed by a popular rising, the people, provoked by the extortions of the Kara-Khitan tax-collectors, surrounding him in his house and pulling it down on top of him. The Uighur *Idikut* took advantage of the rising to send messengers to Chingis offering him allegiance and submission. As we have seen, he was rewarded with one of the great Khan's own daughters.

The Gurkhan was now menaced with revolt on all sides. In such circumstances he accepted the appearance of Kuchluk as a happy chance. The refugee was cordially received at court, given a princess as wife and made into the right hand of the Gurkhan. Kuchluk, a Nestorian Christian himself, adopted the Buddhist faith of his wife and flung himself with true nomad ferocity into the task of subduing the Gurkhan's rebel subjects. Nestorian priests were crucified on the Church doors, Moslem mullahs hanged outside their mosques, and a reign of terror declared throughout the land.

Kuchluk was a man of great ambition. He had been bitterly opposed to his own father's weak defensive policy against the Mongols and it was he who had nursed Jamuga among the Naiman as a weapon to be used against Chingis. Driven from his own country by the Mongol victory, he sought to win an empire for himself in East Turkestan by treachery against the host who had given him refuge and a great position. Within a few months of his establishment at the Kara-Khitan court he was intriguing with the powerful Khwarizm-Shah, Mohammed, the Gurkhan's greatest rival in Central Asia.

The story of the Khwarizmian Empire must be told in the next chapter. The shahs, however, had by now succeeded to almost the whole of the vast Seljukid Empire and were masters of most of Turan and Iran, the lands of Turks and Iranians. When Mohammed cast off the Gurkhan's suzerainty in 1208, it was a challenge which could hardly be ignored. The Khwarizm-Shah was an able man, a victorious conqueror, and he was quick to see the advantage he might win by posing as the champion of Islam in Central Asia. The Moslem merchants, sorely distressed by the confusion on the great trade-routes through the infidel Kara-Khitan territory, as well as by the persecution of their fellow-religionists in Kashgaria, were only too anxious to assist. Mohammed was as unscrupulous as he was ambitious and it did not very much concern him that Kuchluk was the chief agent of the persecution of the Moslems in the Gurkhan's territories. It was much more important that Kuchluk was willing, at a price, to betray his friend and master.

When the inevitable war broke out in 1210 between the Gurkhan and Mohammed, Kuchluk rose in the rear of the Kara-Khitan army, pillaged the treasury at Uzgand and threatened the capital at Balasagun. The Gurkhan, caught between two fires, found even the gates of his own capital closed against him, and, though he managed to take the city by assault, he became the prisoner of the treacherous Kuchluk a few months later.

The same year, 1211, the first Mongol squadrons sent by the all-knowing and ever-watchful Chingis, appeared in Northern Semirechiye, to observe and report on the revolutions which had followed the appearance of the Merkit and Naiman fugitives in the empire of Kara-Khitai. When the Chinese campaign closed in 1215 Chingis was splendidly informed of the position in Central Asia, partly because of his own information service, partly from the fact that he had received ambassadors at Peking the year before from the Khwarizm-Shah. The rise of Kuchluk was a bad omen, for the Naiman prince now had not only a settled base in a rich country, but he was in a position to do infinite harm to the trade-relations between China and Central Asia.

Chingis was now master of the greater part of Northern China, and he had subdued, though not broken, the Tangut kingdom which commanded the Lop Nor caravan routes. All the Turkish and Mongol tribes of Siberia and the Far East had submitted to him, and it was intolerable that the treacherous and vindictive Kuchluk should be able to threaten his communications with the West. The Uighur and Moslem merchants were no doubt active in pressing upon him the need to meet this menace, for when at last the Mongol squadrons rode into Kashgaria under the command of Jebei-Noyon, they brought with them not only the terror of their bows and swords, but a political wisdom which was matchless in its cunning effectiveness. The policy of Jebei in Kashgaria could only have been worked out by men who knew perfectly the situation in the Kara-Khitan Empire and it is safe to assume that it was adopted on the advice of the Moslem and Uighur merchants and officials whom Chingis had now gathered round him in great numbers.

In 1218 Jebei with two divisions crossed the frontiers of Kara-

Khitai, proclaiming freedom of faith to all. This was equivalent to proclaiming also security of trade and of the person, so that Kuchluk's subjects rose against him on all sides. In a few months the wretched man was overtaken in Badakshan and put to death. The Mongols were now looked upon by the Moslems as liberators, while their prestige grew enormously, for, as Vladimirtsov points out, two Mongol divisions had accomplished in a few months what the mighty Khwarizm-Shah had completely failed to do in years.

The Mongol frontiers now ran side by side with those of the Khwarizmian Empire, an empire that ran to the Caspian and Aral Sea, to the Gulf of Persia and the river Indus, the heir to peoples and civilizations older than those of China itself. We have already said that Chingis had no desire for anything but peaceful relations with the West. His task in China was very far from finished and a period of peaceful trade could bring him nothing but advantage. The folly and arrogance of Mohammed, faults which themselves were doubtless aggravated by the internal dissensions in his own empire, decided that the relations between the two powers must be of war and not of peace. The next years were to be occupied with the conquest of Central Asia and Iran, with fabulous cavalry raids over the Caucasus into Europe and back through the Russian steppe. In the end the Mongols, who twenty years before could hardly have known of the existence of any other country save China, were to be established as the rulers of the world from the Pacific to the Hungarian Plains. Had Chingis not turned to the West after his defeat of the Kin it is more than likely that the world would never have heard of him. One more among the many barbarian rulers of Northern China would hardly have been important even for the Chinese, and in world history must have gone unnoticed. Twice before him, Turko-Mongol invasions had set up empires embracing both eastern and western Asia, first the Huns and then the Turks. But in neither case was the empire the work of one man, nor even of one generation, and once formed fell rapidly to pieces, leaving nothing behind. But this genius, who did not even succeed in uniting his own little people till he was fifty years old, before his death had built one of the greatest empires in history and carried out an organizing and creative work which endured for generations and the consequences of which were to be felt for many centuries, so much so that the Mongol invasion of Central Asia may justly be considered one of the great turning-points in world history.

2. The Empire of the Khwarizm-Shah

IN no part of the world does one get the feeling of land so much as in Central Asia. This way, that way, for many thousands of miles you know there is land, the flat grass steppes, rolling sand-dunes, broken ground of crumbling yellow loess covered with sparse scruo, sometimes in the far distance the lofty and solitary white peaks of mountains floating on the dust clouds, but always land and the feeling of land. All the more astonishing therefore, when the very existence of the sea has passed from one's mind, to come quite suddenly upon the sea, to ride over a bare clay ridge and have it stretching before you brilliant in the sun, shining like a mirage. The Aral Sea is only a great salt lake, but once it was a part of a vast inland sea which joined with the Caspian. Into it drain the two great rivers of Central Asia, the Amu and the Syr, or Oxus and Jaxartes as we call them in the West.

Along the estuary of the Amu, amid the many winding channels, here and there shaded with poplar and willow, the wide beds of reeds, the blue lakes, was the ancient province of Khwarizm, the modern Khiva, governed for many centuries by rulers with the title of Khwarizm-Shahs who had their capital at Urganj. One of the great trade-routes from Europe passed round the shores of the Aral Sea to Urganj, and thence up the Amu to join the great Khorasan high road to Samarkand. The Khwarizmians, who included among their subjects the ancestors of the Turkomans, were naturally a trading people and the Khwarizmian merchant in his high lambskin cap was a familiar figure in the markets of all the Central Asian cities.

In the early twelfth century, the Khwarizm-Shahs were the vassals of the great Seljukid Empire with its capital at Rey on the Caspian. The Seljuks at the height of their power ruled over most of Asia Minor and the Middle East, including the wealthy Central Asian provinces of Khorasan and Khwarizm. The tendency of all medieval feudal states, in both Asia and Europe, was to expand horizontally whenever a strong central power was established, a wide extent of vassal territory compensating for the weakness of general productive power. When the vassals were squeezed dry and the central power grew weak, these great empires split up, till some new power should arise to unite all or a part of the old domains under a new dynasty. In Asia this process was greatly complicated by the age-long conflict between the two forms of production, the pastoral nomad and the settled agrarian. In Central Asia this latter conflict was at its most acute for, though the Iranian population, the Tajiks, were settled and highly-cultured agriculturists and town-dwellers, the Turkish peoples were split in two. One portion was settled on the land, traded and lived in towns, the other kept its ancient pastoral life on the steppes and with it retained the military traditions of the Turkish race.

From Nishapur in modern Persia (Iran) to the Oxus was the wealthy and beautiful province of Khorasan, beyond the Oxus, to the Syr, was the province of Soghd, of which the city of Samarkand was the commercial and political centre. Across the river Syr the boundaries of the Seljukid Empire came to an end, guarded by the busy commercial and frontier cities of Otrar and Shash (Tashkent). Across the Syr, from the beginning of the twelfth century was the empire of Kara-Khitai, which at the height of its power ruled for a time up to the Oxus.

Though the inhabitants of Soghd, Khwarizm and Khorasan were mixed between Turanians and Iranians, with Turanians predominating in the first two, the system of administration and civilization in general was Iranian, though greatly complicated by the frequent invasions and conquests of the nomadic and militaristic Turks. Trans-Oxiana, Soghd, was always important for Persia as its chief granary, while the great trade with the nomads was also indispensable to the country's economic life. The nomads sold cattle for slaughter, sheep and pack animals, hides, furs and slaves. The slaves were sometimes domestic, women and boys for the courts and great houses, but just as often military, for service in the armies. In return they received clothing and grain, luxury articles for their feudal chiefs and military leaders. As in China and Russia the chief trade with the nomads was carried on at the frontiers, whither they drove their herds and brought their slaves to market. The great prosperity of Khwarizm was founded very largely on this nomad trade, as well as on its fortunate position upon a great international commercial route.

The first half of the twelfth century in Central Asia history was marked by the weakening and ultimate collapse of the Seljukid dynasty and the rise of the two new powers of the Khwarizm-Shahs and the Gurkhans of Kara-Khitai. In 1128 the Turkish Khwarism-Shah Atsiz succeeded to the governorship of the province of Khorasan, thereby, though still a Seljuk vassal, becoming the real founder of the new dynasty of Khwarizm-Shahs. The Seljuks were themselves of Turkoman descent but this did not save them from a revolt of all their Turkish vassals which finally destroyed their power. Their Sultan Sanjar was defeated in 1141 by the Kara-Khitans, who occupied Bokhara, while the Khwarizm-Shah in his turn seized the chance to declare his independence. Sanjar, after many years of wandering and captivity, died at Merv in 1157.

Till the end of the century the Khwarizm-Shahs had only an uneasy hold over Khorasan and Khwarizm, but in 1194 the Shah Takash, father of Mohammed, slew the last Seljukid sultan, Togrul III, at Rey in Persia, while in the first two decades of the next century the ambitious Mohammed turned on the Kara-Khitans, through the help of the treacherous Kuchluk, and took half their empire from them, conquered Afghanistan, part of which became the fief of his son Jelal ed-Din, and imposed his suzerainty on Irak,[1] Fars and Azerbaijan, becoming the lord of all Iran. At Baghdad a small pontifical Abbasid state maintained only the shadow of the once revered and powerful Caliphate. The semi-independent emir Otman, ruler of Samarkand, husband of Mohammed's daughter, also saw his power destroyed by Mohammed and was actually killed at the demand of his own wife. Whilst Chingis was building his empire in the East, Mohammed had built an even greater empire in the West, succeeding to the domains of the once all-powerful Seljuks, whose last princes were prisoners in his citadel at Urganj.

In the coming clash between the two empires it must have seemed to Mohammed that victory was inevitably his. The Mongols were a small and unknown people, while, though they had certainly defeated the Chinese Kin Emperor, they had not yet destroyed him. Among the wild peoples of the Gobi and the Altai their power might be great, but he had little doubt as to what

[1] This was the Eastern or Persian Irak, as distinct from Mesopotamia, Western or Arabian Itak.

must happen to them if they came into conflict with his own powerful armies, drawn from the great countries of Turan and Iran, with all the tradition of the great past behind them.

But Mohammed, though energetic and unscrupulous, was not a very wise man. He did not understand that his empire was great in name only and that its whole social and political structure was in complete decay, a decay which his conquests had only accelerated. He did not understand that the Mongols, on the other hand, were a young and homogeneous people, with a strong feeling of confidence in their own power which gave to their nomad feudalism a military weapon of the greatest value, and one that was always lacking in their enemies, namely, a high morale. Least of all was he capable of understanding that Chingis, in claiming the protection of the Blue Sky, of heaven itself, was really unconsciously expressing the fact that the Mongols were acting as the armed instrument of the laws of human history.

Central Asian feudal society, as it was formed in the first eight centuries of our era, was based on the landowner, the territorial aristocrat of *dihqan*. There was neither strong central power not all-powerful clergy and the prince was only the chief landowner. The great commercial centres had early developed a wealthy trading class, dependent on the China trade, who possessed vast estates and dwelt on them in fortified castles, the first cause of disintegration of the feudal agricultural state in which the aristocrat was expected above everything to be a good "landlord" (*katkhunda*), to cut canals and underground conduits for irrigation, to build bridges and maintain the public buildings.

Administration was divided into two main categories, the palace offices and the diwan, or chancery, which controlled the chief ministries and government offices. The palace offices were sometimes filled by the ruling families, sometimes by slaves. In course of time the great civil officials, the tax-farmers and collectors, also became landlords and the importance of the territorial aristocracy correspondingly decreased.

The frequent conquests by military nomad powers were the chief cause of the decline of Central Asian society. As each new power arose the importance of the military class increased correspondingly. So also did that of the Moslem clergy who were the monopolists of culture and therefore of the greatest value in running the administrative machine. The military forces were composed largely of slaves and mercenaries and each military commander became the holder of a great fief from which he maintained his men. Apart from the soldiers and the clergy, the rest of the population was looked upon only as a body of taxpayers. War became for those swollen empires an economic necessity, a means for keeping the vast army contented and supplied with luxuries, of maintaining the great courts and paying the handsome interest exacted by the money-lenders.

Money was extremely scarce and the Iranian and Turkish countries never adopted to the same extent the Chinese expedient of inflation. It was because of the scarcity of money that jewels and precious things became of such great economic importance and every war was in a sense a war of plunder. Poets and scholars abounded in medieval Asia, great poets and wonderful scholars, but they were supported and encouraged by the courts not through love of poetry or of learning, but because, like dancing girls and jewels, they were the outward marks of power by which the monarch made visible and manifes this strength. They collected Firdausis and Sa'adis much as a modern millionaire collects contemporary paintings or subsidizes a high-brow publishing business.

The Persians conceived of the ruler as an autocrat who commanded the state. The Turkish conquerors who succeeded the great Iranian dynasties looked upon the empire as the property of the Khan's family, to be divided among its members. So the division of the great empires into semi-independent fiefs and principalities, the rise of the clergy as a powerful political and economic force, the strengthening of the merchants and usurers, finally destroyed the agrarian basis of the old feudal state. The *dihqan*, the landowner, was no longer of any importance by the time of the Mongol invasion and the nation was divided into an army to whom the king gave fiefs, and subjects whom he "defended" from external and internal enemies, requiring in return unconditional obedience and the unmurmuring payment of taxes.

So the irrigation works fell into decay, the agricultural districts grew more and more deserted and famine entered the life of the people of Turkestan also as an enemy equal in power for evil to the ruler and the priest. Barthold gives two interesting quotations which reflect only too exactly how the poor man lived in the empire of the Seljuks and Khwarizm-Shahs. Sultan Sanjar is reported to have said that 'to protect the strong from injury on the part of the weak is more necessary than to protect the weak from the arbitrary actions of the strong, for the insulting of the weak by the strong is only injustice, whereas the insulting of the strong by the weak is both injustice and dishonour. If the masses are to emerge from subjection the result will be complete disorder, the lesser will perform the duties of the great, but the great cannot carry out the duties of the lesser.' In an official document of Sanjar's time an even more characteristic pronouncement on the class of 'artisans and agriculturists' is to be found. 'They do not know the language of kings, and any idea of agreeing with their rulers or of revolting against them is beyond them; all their efforts are devoted to one aim, to acquire the means of existence and maintain wife and children; obviously they are not to be blamed for this, and for enjoying constant peace.'

When the holy man Ch'ang Ch'un reached Turkestan the first thing he remarked was the peasant patiently irrigating his field of barley. The second was the fields of cotton. The digging of that narrow trench in the yellow, clayey earth, the endless waiting for the rain which will fill it with muddy water, the careful cultivation of the field to win the means of life for himself, his wife and children, this was certainly the main concern of the Central Asian peasant. But life was becoming ever harder to maintain. The growth of commerce with the nomads meant that more land had to be given up to cotton, to provide them with the ropes, clothes and materials they needed, and so ever increased the danger of famine when the burden of war and taxation made it impossible to buy food.

'It is here they make the stuff called *tu-lu-ma*,' wrote Ch'ang Ch'un's disciple when they reached Almalik, 'which gave rise to the popular story about a material made from "sheep's wool planted in the ground." We now procured seven pieces of it to make into winter clothes. In appearance and texture it is like Chinese willow-down—very fine, soft and clean. Out of it they make thread, ropes, cloth and wadding. The farmers irrigate their fields with canals; but the only method employed by the people of these parts for drawing water is to dip a pitcher and carry it on the head. Our Chinese buckets delighted them. "You Chinese are so clever at everything!" they said.'

The language of kings, then as now, of which these diligent peasants were so woefully ignorant, was the language of the bandit dressed in the trappings of state. It was wrong, however, of Sanjar's minister to assume that the quiet husbandmen, so very like their own cattle in the eyes of their rulers, had no idea of revolt against their rulers. Khorasan and Soghd were full of armed bands living in the mountains or on the frontiers, raiding villages and sacking caravans, landless men who called themselves 'warriors of the Faith,' cloaking their struggle under a religious guise, a kind of free Cossack brotherhood. Their leaders were the ruined landowners, or artisans from the towns, even minor clerics from the colleges of Bokhara or Samarkand. For just as the land, by ceasing to support the tiller any longer, created the landless brigand, so the great towns were also full of sedition among the unemployed officials, the artisans who felt the oppression of the great merchants and tax-collectors, and even the small class of wage-earners and journeymen. The Moslem rising in Bokahra against the Kara-Khitans was led by an artisan.

Mohammed in his war against the Kara-Khitans came forward as the champion of Islam. In doing so he caused his interests to coincide with those of the masses in Bokhara and Samarkand, oppressed by the plundering extortions of the infidel Kara-Khitan tax-collectors. The democratic Moslem movement which had already broken out in Bokhara and gave Mohammed the occasion to lead his armies through to battle with the Gurkham, spread also to East Turkestan where Chingis took much cleverer advantage of it. The defeat of the Kara-Khitans by Mohammed, however, only exchanged an infidel oppressor for one of the true faith and soon the Kwarizmians in their tall lamb-skin caps were the most hated sight in Central Asia. In some districts they held all the land, while in the towns their exactions exasperated the people to breaking-point. In 1212 the people of Samarkand massacred every Khwarizmian they could lay hands on, hanging up their carcases in the bazaar for butcher's meat.

Mohammed took a fearful revenge, drowning every insurrection against his rule in rivers of blood. The fact that his subjects hated him and were in rebellion was not in itself, however, sufficient to make his empire unstable. The other civilized countries of the world at the time were no different from the Khwarizmian empire in this respect. The full rottenness of society was shown in the complete inability of the ruling classes to agree among themselves as to the division of the plunder extorted from the people and the foreign enemy.

The Khwarizm-Shah was in a state of open enmity with the Caliph at Baghdad, the religious head of Islam, and therefore forfeited the confidence of the clergy. Jealous of the power of the clergy, Mohammed caused the head of the great Hanefite sect at Bokhara, Madjd ed-Din, the brother of the Vizir Nidham el-Molk, to be murdered. Estates were confiscated on the mere suspicion of heresy and the clergy gradually driven to supporting the military party, whose head was Turkan Khatun, the Shah's mother.

The court maintained a horde of spies throughout the country and men were exiled and murdered on the slightest suspicion of opposition to the Sultan. 'Fie upon this treacherous world,' exlaims the pious Nesawi in his life of Sultan Jelal ed-Din, 'in which one dares not pronounce the funeral eulogy of a man treacherously assassinated, or even utter his name! Woe to those men who become attached to this dwelling in which great desires cannot be realized!' It was Nesawi who wrote that the mark of a truly great cleric was to consider this world as an atom of dust floating in the midst of the other planets, or rather as a simple, imperceptible point among the other points of space. Yet he tells us that the great priest who reached this conception of the immateriality of life was a man of immense wealth, estates and farms, with no less than 6,000 law students and jurisconsults attendant upon him.

Power in the empire was in fact divided between Mohammed and his cruel, clever old mother, Turkan Khatun, who lived in the family palace at Urganj, continually intriguing with the military leaders and priests against her own son Mohammed and his son Jelal ed-Din. 'At the time when she had achieved the height of her greatness,' writes Nesawi, 'she was given the title of Khodavend Jihan, that is "Mistress of the Universe.' . . . She decided all litigious matters brought to her with wisdom and equity and always did justice to the oppressed against the oppressor. Yet she allowed herself to be drawn into shedding blood very easily. Her country owed her a number of charitable works. . . . She had seven great and distinguished lords as secretaries. Whenever two different decisions on any matter were arrived at, one hers and one the Sultan's, it was always the one dated last which was operated, and without regard to its authorship.'

Nesawi's polite phrases conceal the bitter poltical struggle which in fact divided the rulers of Khwarizmia, a struggle upon which Chingis was fully informed and of which he took immediate advantage. Turkan Khatun, not content with fighting her son, bitterly hated and persecuted Jelal ed-Din, the only one of the royal princes with any kind of ability. Jelal, a very dark, small man. Turkish in his speech and manners, full of a swaggering fiery energy, was the son of Mohammed by a Turkish prostitute who had won his royal favour. Into his hands was to fall the task of organizing the national resistance of the Iranian peoples to the Mongol invasion. How little capable he was of this we shall see later.

3. Cities and Caravans

SOGHDIANA, the province of which Samarkand was the commercial and Bokhara the religious capital, was counted by the Moslems as one of the four earthly paradises. The upper waters of the river Soghd (the modern Zarafshan, 'gold scatterer'), run through high, steep hills, covered with villages, bringing wealth and fertility to the plains below.

Samarkand stands at the junction of the main trade-routes from India (via Balkh in Afghanistan), from Persia (via Merv) and from the Turkish dominions. Its origin is almost legendary, though there is reason to believe that it was founded by Alexander of Macedon, and the region of which it is the centre has always been famous for its great fertility. Like all the cities of Central Asia it consisted of two towns, an inner town with a citadel and the outer suburbs. The site of the Shahristan, the inner town, in the time of the Mongol invasion, was on the place called Afrasiyab, north of the modern city. The Shahristan had four gates, and from the Chinese gate the road ran down to the river, crossing it by a bridge which was covered by floods when the snow melted in the mountains in the spring.

The outer town was a series of wide-spreading and beautiful suburbs, an area of forty-four square miles enclosed by a wall of earth twenty-seven miles long. The irrigation system of the city was one of the most perfect in the world, consisting of eight main ariqs, or canals, with 680 sluices. Water was brought into almost every house and the main ariqs were lined with lead. Practically every house had its garden with fruit-trees, while the stately cypresses and elms of Samarkand were famous throughout Asia. The cool public squares were shaded by cypress-trees cut into astonishing figures of animals by the fantasy of the citizens. There were no less than 2,000 places in the stone-paved streets and squares where iced water could be obtained free, kept in copper cisterns and earthenware vessels, or spouting freshly from the fountains.

Viewed from the citadel the town was a green mass of trees and gardens, with almost no houses to be seen, though at least 100,000 families were living there. In the very early morning a marvellous view over the gardens to the lovely majesty of the mountains could be seen, but as the heat grew and the dust rose the view was obscured, only the tips of the snowy peaks sometimes appearing above what appeared to be a cloud but was really the dust from the plains.

Samarkand was as old an industrial city as it was a market. The famous silk and cotton fabrics of the Zarafshan valley, the arms and metal articles of Ferghana, where coal was mined, were sold in its bazaars. But the city itself was famous for its paper manufacture, an art learned from Chinese craftsmen taken prisoner in 751. Sir Aurel Stein has established that pure rag paper was made in China as early as the second century A.D., but Samarkand was for long the only paper-making centre outside China itself. Satins and coloured fabrics, large copper vessels, artistic goblets, tents, stirrups, bridleheads and straps, the sweet melon packed with snow in leaden moulds, were all exported from this city of gardens.

Bokhara, which has always occupied its present site, was remarkable for its mosques, colleges and castles and carpet industry. The wide streets were paved with stone, but travellers remarked that the city was overcrowded, suffered from frequent fires, had bad water and was smelly. Its piety and learning grew, in fact, in direct relation to its dirt and overcrowding. No doubt much of the latter was due to the many thousand students who flocked there from all over Asia to study law, dialectic, and the sermons of the most famous preachers. Despite the lofty philosophical structures of these last, it is to be feared that their form was often a matter of greater concern that their content and that monkish humour played no little part in their elaborations. Nesawi, pious and bookish though he is, tells with evident relish of a successful bet made by one great priest to another that he would upset his rival's delivery of his sermon and cause him to stop short in embarrassment. Certainly, if the mass of poor students starved and were content with a stoney corner of the college, the wealthy clerics and officials could be sure of such a meal each day, save during the great fasts, as would please the palate of the strictest epicure, for the meats and melons of Bokhara were as famous as the gardens of Samarkand.

Shash (Tashkent) was the centre of the great arms industry of Central Asia, making high saddles of horse hide or wild asses' skin, quivers, tents, cloaks, swords and metal-work, while both here and at Otrar great trade was done with the nomads. Horses, furs, hides and slaves, were the products the nomads sold chiefly on the bazaars here along the river Syr. Down the Amu, through the wealthy oasis country of Khwarizum, came the products of the southern steppes of Russia and the Turkish nomads south of the river Ural. Sable, miniver, ermines, fox-furs, martens, beavers, spotted hares, all the produce of the hunt across the great plains came here. The bazaars traded briskly in wax, arrows, birch bark, high fur caps, fish glue, fish teeth, horse hides, honey, falcons, swords, armour, sheep and cattle, and lastly, the white-skinned, blue-eyed Slavonic slaves. Khwarizm was also famous for its bows, which only the strongest could bend, and its carpets and cloth fabrics.

From Samarkand to Bokhara the road was known as the Royal Road. Thence the highway went through Khorasan, with one branch passing through Merv, another dividing off at the Castle of the Winds to Herat. Herat, just before the Mongol invasion, was considered by one Arab traveller to be the richest city he had ever seen. Its mills were turned by wind, it had 12,000 shops in its markets, 6,000 hot baths and 659 colleges, while the population was over 400,000. Most famous city of all was Nishapur, the capital of Khorasan, famed for its healthy climate, its rose gardens and prosperity. Every day the caravans brought in great stores of merchandise for its wealthy merchants and as a manufacturing centre it was without a rival in the Moslem world.

These were the cities which were the foundation of the wealth of Asia and the power of the Kharizm-Shah. This busy trade was of immense value and importance and the interests of their merchants could not be disregarded. In running counter to those interests Mohammed undoubtedly brought about the downfall of his unstable empire and made certain the victory of the Mongols, though at a terrible cost to the prosperity of Middle Asia. In order to understand quite clearly why this was so, it is necessary to examine a little into the mechanism of Asiatic trade.

We are accustomed to think of a caravan as a thing of pure

romance, whereas in fact it was (and is) a considerable commercial venture, of which the equivalent in modern history is the convoys of East and West Indiamen which first brought wealth to the merchant class of our own island and built up the prosperity of Bristol, Liverpool and London. 'Trade with distant lands,' writes Barthold, 'with Russia and China, brought the merchants great advantages, but was connected with considerable credit, and the temporary 'with Russia and China, brought the merchants great advantages, but was connected with considerable risk, since goods in the East were always taken on credit, and the temporary cessation of trade therefore caused the merchants great harm. During the campaign of one of the Seljuk sultans on Trebizond the cessation of trade between Greece and Russia caused great loss to the Mussulman merchants. When in the year of the battle of Kalka the cutting of the means of communication with South Russia for a short time stopped the transport of fox furs, squirrels, beavers and other goods, this fact was of such importance for the Mussulmans that Ibn Athir specially notices it. The armistice between the Khwarizm-Shah and the Kara-Khitans (probably in 1209), at once led to the sending of a trading caravan to East Turkestan. The poet Sa'adi visited Kashgar with this caravan. At the commencement of the twelfth century the overland trade with China had still greater importance than formerly, since maritime trade was interrupted by an accidental circumstance, that is by the dispute between the owners of the two harbours in the Persian Gulf, Ormuz and Kish. Each of them endeavoured in every way to stop merchants sailing from the other's harbour. On the other hand, after Mohammed's campaign against the Kipchaks and the annexation of the northern half of Semirechiye (Jeti-su) to the Mongol Empire, the Khwarizm-Shah's state began to abut directly on Chingis-Khan's, while both conquerors, particularly the latter, tried to establish security in their dominions.'

To send a caravan to China, or across the Russian steppes to Central Asia, meant more than a big investment in goods. The troubled political conditions and the general corruption of the officials in Mohammed's empire compelled the hire of an expensive escort and often considerable bribes to court officials. Nesawi, who was appointed to a high office in the Chancellery of the Sultan Jelal ed-Din, reveals what this meant in terms of hard cash. 'One day alone, when the Sultan was away, my office in the Chancellery brought me in over 1,000 dinars (£500). Other days, whilst more modest, my profits stayed at a very reasonable level, so I did not waste any time before vigorously resisting all those who disputed my place.'

Business was conducted on credit largely because money was always so exceedingly short. Apart from the merchants, bankers, great lords, clerics and officials, very few of the population ever handled money at all. Great sums were squeezed into the treasury by taxation and the profits of trade were immense, but nevertheless the shortage of money and precious stones was always one of the great difficulties of commerce and the State in the Middle Ages. Nesawi notes it as a remarkable thing that Mohammed was able to make his conquests without depriving his women of their jewels. When Kuchluk took the Gurkhan prisoner, Mohammed was greatly annoyed because he thereby lost the Gurkhan's daughter and dowry, and because Kuchluk had taken 'the precious stones and other things of price the latter possessed and had collected in the course of ages in different countries.'

The cause of this was the great shortage of commodities arising from the inability of the weak productive system to meet the demand and aggravated by the constant wars and the ever-growing luxury of the feudal courts. The nomads, poverty-stricken in their steppe, did not feel a greater need for goods than did these great lords of ancient civilizations, and whereas the nomads, free from the usurer and content till now with simple exchange, could always rob when all else failed, the great rulers of the Asiatic states, while robbing continually both the external and internal enemy, were also compelled to buy and sell, and were at the mercy of the rapidly growing merchants' and usurers' capitalist class.

Mr Owen Lattimore, in his book *The Desert Road to Turkestan* has described a scene in a caravanserai on the Chinese frontier which is true also for all Asia in the thirteenth century. 'I was lodged in a caravanserai around whose court were the quarters of a score of traders, bankers and brokers. Here again I was thrown among men whose talk was for ever of the prices of wool and camels, of caravan rates and cart hire, of journeys counted in many tens of days from Pao-t'ou into the remote hinterland of Asia, and of the bandits besetting this road or the soldiers obstructing that. Or else their gossip would run on storms and the loss of caravans, or lucky ventures that had made men rich at one blow, and all the chances and alarms of a way of trading and living utterly different from the alien civilization which I had seen creeping up along the railway, but of which they seemed so little aware.' The same conversation, making variations for the method of transport, could no doubt have been heard in any eighteenth-century coffee-house frequented by the captains of East Indiamen. The life of the caravan on its long journeying was as self-contained as that of the Indiaman. The rare towns were the ports, landfall and departure on that vast ocean of steppe and desert had their counterpart, winds and storms were no less terrible and to be feared than at sea, and the lore of the camel-driver was as rich and varied as that of the able seaman.

What it meant to travel with one of these great caravans, how essentially commercial and unromantic it was in times of peace, we may know from the memoirs of the Florentine Francis Balducci Pegolotti, a factor in the service of the great Florentine house of the Bardi. Pegolotti wrote his handbook for merchants using the land-route to Cathay about 1340, when the descendants of Chingis had made the route the safest in the world. The caravans then started from Tana on the Sea of Azov and the first stage was by ox- or horse-wagon to Astrakhan. This was ten or twelve days by horse-wagon, twice as long by ox; then the route went up the Volga to Sarai, from there to the mouth of the river Ural by water, then across the desert by camel-wagon to Urganj, some thirty days in all. Goods could be readily sold there, after which began the next long stage to Otrar in camel-wagons, thirty-five or forty days in all. From Otrar the caravan went to Almalik on the Ili and thence to Kanchu to the Grand Canal was forty-five days on horseback and then the journey was completed by water.

Pegolotti's instructions are curious. 'Let your beard grow long and do not shave. At Tana take a dragoman and do not try to save money on a bad one. Also two good menservants. And if the merchant likes to take a woman with him from Tana he can do so; if he does not like to take one there is no obligation, only if he does take one he will be kept much more comfortably than if he does not take one. Howbeit, if he do take one, it will be well that she be acquainted with the Turkish tongue as well as the men.'

Pegolotti then estimates the amount to be taken for a good trading-venture and what will be the costs. Taking the gold florin or ducat at 9s. 6d. the value of the merchandise will be nearly £12,000 and the cost of the journey from £140 to £190 going and nearing £12 a head on his beasts coming back. £2 10s. 0d. bought from twelve to twenty pounds of Cathay silk.

If this was the sum involved when one merchant made a modest venture, we can imagine the vast sums locked up in such a caravan as that great train of 500 camels which the four merchants led to Otrar from the dominions of Chingis. Of course, between the conditions described by Pegolotti, when no escort was needed and the roads were perfectly safe, and the conditions when the Khwarizm-Shah misruled the whole of the lands of Turan and Iran, there is no comparison. All the more reason then, that the far-sighted merchants should turn with a sigh of relief towards the iron discipline of the Mongol Army and the organizing genius of Chingis-Khan. 'The interests of Chingis-Khan,' Barthold says truly, 'coincided fully with the interests of the Mussulman capitalists. There was no similar harmony between the political aspirations of Mohammed and the interests of the merchants in his state.'

Not only was Mohammed acting against the deepest interests of his own State when he ventured on an adventurous and aggressive policy against Chingis, but he was doing so when that State was so torn and riven that he had absolutely no hope of success. Barthold sums up the position perfectly when he says that 'Mohammed therefore could not depend on a single element of the administrative system, nor on a single class of the population. The issue of the struggle between such a power and the fresh forces of the nomads, united at this time under one of the most talented organizers of all ages, is comprehensible.'

PART V

The Conquest of the West

1. The Plan of Genius

IN 1215 an embassy with a caravan from the Khwarizm-Shah reached Chingis in Peking. It is not altogether clear what was Mohammed's purpose in opening relations with the Mongols. Professor Barthold was of the opinion that he was from the first not desirous of peaceful commercial relations with the new power in the Far East. It is possible, for the Khwarizmian merchants, who reached the Mongol camp near Kara-Korum the following year, seem to have imagined that they were among ignorant barbarians whom they could cheat as they pleased. They were rucely brought to their senses when they put extravagant prices on their goods and discovered to their cost that the Mongols had an excellent commercial sense.

The Persian historian Juzjani writes frankly that Mohammed's embassy and caravan were nothing but an intelligence mission sent out when news reached him of the conquest of the Kin by the new nomadic power. 'He was desirous of investigating, by means of trustworthy persons of his own, the truth of this statement, and to bring certain information respecting the condition and amount of the Mughal forces and their weapons and war-like apparatus.' One of Mohammed's ministers in later years related to Juzjani that he was constantly making inquiry respecting the Kin states and questioned all comers about them, being ambitious to rule there, despite the representation of his servants. Whether Mohammed really dreamed of extending his empire to China, we may well doubt. Yet it is true enough that the only hope of keeping the shaky structure together at all was through war and he was certainly preparing forcibly to absorb his former ally Kuchluk when Jebei's squadrons anticipated him.

In 1216 troops of the Khwzrizm-Shah made an expedition against the Kipchak nomads in the northern steppes beyond the Syr Daria. Here they made contact for the first time with the Mongol cavalry who had occupied Northern Semirechiye, and carried their pursuit of the sons of Toktoa, the Merkit chief, into the Turgai steppe. There was slight skirmishing between the two forces, but the Mongols avoided serious conflict, strictly confining themselves to observation.

So Chingis was well aware with whom he was dealing when the ambassadors reached him. Yet he hoped for friendly relations, and, what is even more important, greatly needed the establishment of normal trade with his Western neighbour. The long and bloody war in Northern China had exhausted the people and ruined the land, while the Mongol armies had taken away all the available movable wealth. Corn was coming in from the settlements along the Yenesei, but it was more than desirable that trade should be resumed with the West by the overland route. The maritime route was blocked by the dispute between the rulers of the two ports of Ormuz and Kish, in the Persian Gulf. The merchants from Khwarizmia, Samarkand and Bokhara, must make a long northerly detour owing to the confusion caused by Kuchluk in East Turkestan and Kashgar. Everything called for the establishment of peace with the Khwarizm-Shah, just as it was necessary to deal violently and effectively with Kuchluk.

So the embassy was well received. 'Say ye unto the Khwarizm-Shah,' Chingis told the ambassadors, 'that I am the sovereign of the sun-rise, and thou the sovereign of the sunset. Let there be between us a firm treaty of friendship, amity and peace, and let traders and caravans on both sides come and go, and let the precious products and ordinary commodities which may be in my territory be conveyed by them into thine, and those of thine, in the same manner, let them bring into mine.'

Chingis sent ambassadors in return to the Khwarizm-Shah, followed by a caravan. Ibn Athir remarks that the Mongols sent their caravan with the particular aim 'to buy materials for clothes,' confirming the impression that the conquest of China, while it had brought wealth to the poor nomads of the steppe, had nevertheless, owing to the stubborn Chinese resistance and consequent devastation, not yet provided them with all they needed, for conquest meant also slaves and concubines to clothe and feed, great estates to be maintained and armies to be equipped.

So, while the squadrons of Jebei-Noyon were pursuing the wretched Kuchluk into the mountains of Badakshan, that land of high-bred and lovely horses, the embassy of Chingis-Khan made its long way to the court of the Khwarizm-Shah, followed by a rich caravan. The Mongol caravan was a trading enterprise of the Moslem merchants who now surrounded Chingis, men from Otrar, Samarkand and Bokhara. Its 500 camels carried nuggets of gold, silver, silks, both the coarse woven kind and precious red fabrics, raw silk, the furs of beaver and sable and many elegant and ingenious articles of Chinese workmanship.

The Khwarizm-Shah received the ambassadors, most of whom were Moslems from his own lands, coldly, affecting to believe himself insulted by the mode of address used by Chingis. How his mind was working we may see from the fact that he privily summoned one of the ambassadors, a native of Bokhara, to his presence and questioned him closely as to the truth of the stories spread about Chingis and the power of his army. In the end he offered the man a great bribe to become his spy. While these unsatisfactory negotiations were going on terrible things were taking place in Otrar, the important frontier city near to Tashkent.

The local governor, whether or not with the knowledge of his master we shall never know, laid violent hands upon the caravan, massacring merchants, guards and camel drivers and taking its rich burden for himself. It is hard to believe that Mohammed was ignorant of this treacherous stupidity. At least he gave the governor his fullest support when it had been committed. Four hundred and fifty men and four great merchants from Otrar, Maragha in Azerbaijan, Bokhara and Herat, perished in the massacre. Though the alarm and anger in commercial circles must have been great, for the destruction of such a caravan meant a loss equivalent to the failure of a great modern trust, Chingis kept his head. Another embassy was sent to demand satisfaction and the punishment of the governor.

The head of the mission was murdered by Mohammed's orders and the other ambassadors grossly insulted. Despite the warnings he had received from every adviser whom he had ever consulted on the power and strength of Chingis the Khwarizm-Shah was decided on war, and it is hard to believe that the decision had not been taken long ago, perhaps even at the time of the despatch of the mission to Peking. For all that, the preparations of the aggressors were pitifully inadequate. From the first, despite their immensely superior forces, they decided to wage a defensive war, but in that kingdom of decay nothing could be accomplished. The order to complete the fortification of Samarkand was never properly fulfilled, while the mass levy, ordered in 1219, had not been completed in the spring of 1220, when the Mongol armies were already across the Syr, marching on Samarkand.

Chingis made his usual thorough preparations for the coming war. His ban was sent out to all Mongol princes and nobles, as well as to the vassal rulers. Of the latter, the Tangut king alone refused men for the levy, against his better judgment, thereby committing a mistake he was to rue bitterly in a few years' time. When the *kuriltai* was assembled the plan of campaign was put before them, discussed and approved. Then began the march over the Atlai to the concentration point on the Irtysh. Yeliu Ch'uts'ai, who was with the army, marvelled at the beauty of the northern slopes of these mountains, where 'the pines and larch are so high, that they seem to reach heaven. The valleys are all abounding in grass and flowers. Ice and snow are in the high places, even in summer.'

To allow of the passage of their artillery train of mangonels and catapults, the product of the Chinese campaign which had added greatly to their technique, the Mongols had to fell trees and make roads through the difficult mountain passes, often sleeping at night on the snow, wrapped in their wet and stinking sheepskins and taking the warmth from their animals. Juchi, the Khan's eldest son, covered the secret concentration of the marching columns at the rendezvous in the steppes east of Lake Balkash. By a swift raid to the lower reaches of the Syr he distracted the enemies' attention and, by a retirement as quick as his thrust, he laid waste the trough of country between the Ak-Kum desert, and the Ala-Tau and Kara-Tau Mountains.

Jelal ed-Din, the son of the Khwarizm-Shah, was swift in pursuit of the raiders, but they had already accomplished their mission, driven off all the horses and forage from this district and made it impossible for an army to advance to disturb the Mongol concentration. A rearguard battle took place, from which the Mongols disengaged themselves in the night by the old ruse of leaving their camp-fires burning and then setting fire to the prairie grass.

It is a legend that the Mongols invaded Asia with an innumerable horde. A quarter of a million men are given to Chingis by Dr Harold Lamb, and other estimates are greater still. Sixty thousand men had been left in China with Mukuli to carry on the war against the Kin. Not more than 70,000 of the Mongol regular army can have fought in the Turkestan campaign, though to these we must add the levies from the subject Turkish peoples, perhaps the same number again. How many were opposed to them it is hard to judge. No doubt in theory the Khwarizm-Shah could have put more than 300,000 soldiers in the field, though in fact it seems doubtful whether he actually succeeded in mobilizing more than 250,000.

By Lake Balkash Chingis prepared his army for the offensive. The difficult march over the Atlai and the Tien Shan ranges had exhausted men and beasts, and the rest which Juchi's raid allowed them was needed. As they got back their strength in the late summer and autumn of 1219 and the different columns took up the positions assigned to them, news came in of the Khwarizm-Shah's preparations. Intelligence is the key to victory and Chingis was always perfectly informed of his enemies' movements. Nor did he look at warfare in any narrow way as a mere act of violence between contending armies. His plans were always the result of deep political insight and he used the political weapon as successfully as the bow and spear. The approach of the Mongols brought with it the usual crop of desertions from the enemy, usually from the official and merchant classes, who gave the Khan the fullest information on the Khwarizmian preparations, also enlightening him on the feud between Mohammed and his mother, Turkan-Khatun, the leader of the military party in the State, information of which he made the fullest use when he had crossed the Syr.

The Shah adopted the cordon system, stringing out his men in packets to guard the crossings of the Syr, sacrificing the advantage of his superior numbers and losing with it the sense of security and mobility. Against an enemy like the Mongols this meant to doom oneself to defeat before the war had started.

The plan worked out by Chingis must always remain one of the most brilliant in the history of warfare, as perfectly executed as it was conceived, thereby differing greatly from another historic and brilliant plan, that of the German General Staff for the invasion of France as it was originally formulated in 1905. In the spring of 1220 Jebei with his two divisions (20,000 men), advancing from Kashgar into the fair and fertile province of Ferghana, marched straight on Khojend, the fortress covering the southern end of the Syr Daria line, thus threatening the right flank of the enemy by a blow aimed at his two great centres of population and political strength in Samarkand and Bokhara.

Jebei's march was meant as a feint and succeeded perfectly. Meanwhile, the main force was distributed into three armies, two of these, under the royal princes Juchi and Jagatai, consisting each of three tumans (divisions of 10,000 men) and the third, designed to deliver the decisive blow, made up of three tumans and the division of the guard, commanded by Chingis himself, his youngest son Tuli and Subodai. This force moved rapidly over the devastated area in a swift flank move to turn the line of the Syr. Every ten horsemen were given three half-grown sheep, cooked and dried, and a skin of water. As they marched they drove their herds of remount horses before them.

At the Syr the armies of the two princes turned south, mopping up the packets of Khwarizmian troops in the fortresses and drawing their reserves into action, aiming at making a junction with Jebei, who had already taken Khojend, and then marching together on Samarkand. Chingis himself, with his army of manoeuvre, crossed the river near Otrar, leaving his rear and the fortresses to the care of his sons, and disappeared completely into the desert of Kizil-Kum. Then at the end of February the Mongols, having made a successful desert march guided by a Turkoman prisoner, debouched on Nur-ata almost on top of Bokhara and in the rear of the Shah's armies. Such a march through the desert would have been impossible at any other season of the year.

At one blow the Shah found his whole line turned and his communications with Khorasan, whose tardy forces had not yet arrived, cut. He fled in panic and on April 11th Chingis rode into Bokhara without resistance. The garrison was cut down as it fled and only the citadel held out for a few days longer. They had captured the city only just in time, their horses exhausted by the long desert march, and the Khan's first order was to fling open the store-houses to feed his horses and men. The Mongol troopers fetched out the musicians and dancers and made merry in the great and holy city of Bokhara, before the eyes of the learned men of its colleges, of the shocked and reverend clerics. A contribution was levied on the city, its merchants and rich men compelled to give up their buried wealth, a great part of it was burned down, and then, driving the wretched inhabitants before them, the Mongols turned east to Samarkand.

That city of gardens and palaces, caught between the hammer

of the royal princes and the anvil of the great Khan, was unable to resist. When the Mongols joined forces under its walls, Chingis's first act was to detach Subodai and Jebei with 30,000 men to pursue Mohammed, the beginning of what was to prove the most remarkable cavalry raid in all history. The gates of the town were opened to the Mongols by the clerics, anxious to save their skins, and the citadel, after a desperate resistance, soon fell. The inhabitants had to submit to massacre and plunder, only the numerous artisans being safe. The latter were enslaved and sent back to East Turkestan and Mongolia, founding little towns and settlements in the valleys of the Ili and Tarim, where they busied themselves in making the war equipment and munitions for the Mongol armies, or articles of luxury for the Mongol nobility.

The Turkish resistance to the Mongol invasion was a desperate but ill-organized struggle. Otrar, where Mohammed had concentrated his best forces, held out for some months, and the governor, Gair-Khan, who knew the fate which awaited him, refused to surrender even when further resistance was hopeless. He fought till all his men were killed or taken, till his own weapons were broken and he could only stand alone and fling stones from the heights of the citadel at his enemies. He was taken alive and executed by Chingis. At Khojend the commander of the fortress, Timur Melik, dug himself in on an island in the river and made a brave and brilliant resistance. The Mongols used the Tajik (Iranian) population to carry stone from the mountains to make a causeway out to the island, bombarded his position with flaming oil and heavy stones from their catapults, but could not make an impression. The garrison escaped on boats, was trapped by Juchi's army further down the river, and took to the steppe, hotly pursued by the Mongols. In the end Timur alone escaped to join the forces of Jelal ed-Din and carry on the fight against the infidel invaders.

The first stage of the campaign was over when the armies joined forces at Samarkand, and in this beautiful and desolate city, within sight of the white peaks of the Hindu Kush, Chingis remained in the autumn and winter of 1220, building up his armies and awaiting news from Subodai's raiding force. The Mongols had shown that they were not only brilliant strategists but resourceful engineers and implacable pursuers. They made use of the population of the conquered country in siege works, performing feats of engineering which would have seemed impossible, diverting the course of rivers, building causeways and bridges, making roads, subduing nature where that was necessary in order to destroy an enemy.

Mohammed was unable to put a strong army in the field against them. His son Jelal ed-Din worked desperately to form a manoeuvring force, but only succeeded after the fall of Samarkand, when the issue was already decided. The old national hostility between Turks and Iranian Tajiks was one difficulty, of which Chingis took full advantage. The hatred of Turkan-Khatun, his grandmother, for the young Jelal ed-Din, was yet another obstacle to unity, for she prevented any real help reaching him from Khwarizmia, while her supporters of the Turkish military party were often more inclined to desert to the Mongols than fight. In many places it was the common people, 'the black folk, highway robbers and criminals,' as Rashid describes them, who made the only resistance.

Yet the chief fact in the Mongol favour remains that theirs was an army, highly organized and disciplined, with a firm central command, before which no amount of feudal chivalry or individual courage could avail, nor even the desperate, brave and unorganized resistance of the people themselves who drove out their own oppressors and prepared to sell themselves dearly before accepting these new masters from the East. The leader of this invading army was no mere nomad raider, for he himself had little taste for fighting save when it was necessary, but a military genius such as the world has seldom seen.

Man in his childhood has been compelled to use the weapon of violence, the brutal destruction of war, in order to effect the great changes necessary for his own development. Nor can we be blind to the fact that the successful prosecution of war demands the highest intellectual powers, the greatest effort of will and the most perfect co-ordinating genius of which man is capable. The greatest commanders, for these very reasons, have always therefore been men who were much more than soldiers, men whose terrible genius possessed something legendary and godlike. Among these few world geniuses, alongside Alexander and Napoleon, Chingis takes his place, one of the greatest of those who were at once destroyers and world builders. When Samarkand fell he was already sixty-five.

2. The Flying Wind

CHINGIS could safely rest his men, still exhausted by the terrible desert march, in Samarkand, for there was no army of the enemy in being anywhere which could threaten him. Though half the city was a smouldering ruin, it was well suited to rest these grim fighters, situated as it was in the heart of a green and fertile land. Chingis-Khan himself relaxed in the unaccustomed luxury, amusing his generals with shows of sword swallowers and dancing boys on tight-ropes, drinking and making merry with the defeated Sultan's singing girls. Yet, though discipline was somewhat loosened and in those days a drunken Mongol trooper was probably the commonest sight in all that ravished city, the mind of the conqueror was not resting and his men were never out of hand.

Information came in continually to the staff. Through the Sultan's Vizir, Nidham el-Molk, the Khan was in touch with Turkan-Khatun and that intriguing old woman, though she did not submit to the conqueror, prevented any real help reaching her defeated son. Indeed, the tax-collectors were still bringing in the money for the war, and the men mobilized by the mass levy, each mounted on his Bactrian dromedary, armed and provisioned, had not yet reached their assembling points, when the Mongol armies broke into Bokhara and Samarkand.

Yet there was a danger that either the fugitive Sultan or his son Jelal ed-Din would still collect a formidable army which might prove a serious menace. So in Samarkand the further details of the campaign were worked out by the tired leader, who was also suffering from that curse of the desert horsemen, a painful eye disease. The task of pursuing Mohammed, as we have seen, was given to three divisions commanded by Jebei, Subodai and Takodjar. Chingis gave them most careful and detailed instructions for their astonishing ride. They were not to engage Mohammed if he succeeded in gathering strong forces and prepared to resist, but to halt, send back word and await instructions. All information, however, showed that the Sultan was panic-stricken and unlikely to make a stand. 'Do not return till you have laid hands on him. Though he seek refuge with a few men in the strong hills or gloomy sands, or hide from human eyes like the magic peri, you must swoop upon him like the flying wind.'

The aim was twofold, to exact revenge from the treacherous Sultan for the murder of the ambassador, an unforgivable crime in Mongol eyes, for in their tribal law the person of an ambassador was sacred, and to prevent him from rallying an army in the hinterland of his wide domains. Having accomplished this the raiders were to make a vast circuit over the Caucasus into the Don steppes and then back into Asia through the Kipchak steppe. The aim was clearly to carry out a great reconnaissance to see that no hostile force should gather to attack the rear and communications of the Mongols while they were busy completing their work in Afghanistan and Iran. Wherever submission was made the Mongols were to accept it and leave their own governor and administration for taxation purposes. Whoever resisted was to be put to the sword. Three years was given for the operation, after which the force was to return to the base in Mongolia.

The Khan proposed to secure the rear of his flying column by sending his son Tuli to subdue the great cities of Khorasan, while the princes Juchi, Jagatai and Ogödei marched into Khwarizm to take the capital of Turkan-Khatun. The armies were then to reunite and rest and recruit on their native pastures around Kara-Korum.

The army of pursuit went after Mohammed like a flying wind indeed. Mohammed's forces were all Turks from his mother's tribe and politically opposed to him. They decided to murder him in the night, but news of the conspiracy was carried to the Sultan, who changed his sleeping-place. When he awoke he saw the felt of the tent he had left shot through and through with arrows, so that it resembled nothing so much as a fretful porcupine. With a few faithful men he fled as fast as horse could carry him to Nishapur, doing his best as he went to rouse every city and fortress to a sense of the Mongol danger. In Nishapur he felt himself safe, and, to drive away memory of the wrongs of fate, fell to drinking and merry-making.

Here the messengers each day brought news of the rapid approach of the Mongols, of the surrender of this city or the sacking of that. At last it dawned on the Sultan that he must do something and he began to make arrangements for a stand in the mountains of Luristan while an army of 100,000 infantry was gathered to support him. But it was already too late and the emirs who had promised him support fled while there was still time to save themselves. Harried from town to town, fortress to fortress, attacked by the common people who saw in him only a hated oppressor, the wretched man was driven at last like a frightened hare to the shores of the Caspian. He took a boat to an island, hoping that the sea would prove a kinder protector than the land, deserting his wives and children in a fortress on the mainland. The fortress fell to the impetuous assault of the pursuers and the Mongol cavalry rode their horses into the salt sea for the first time. They did not need to go further in the chase, for Mohammed, when he heard that his wives and children were prisoners and his treasure on its way to Samarkand under convoy, could resist no more. He died of exhaustion and grief, of the utter failure of his will. Before dying he named his younger son Jelal ed-Din Mankoberti, his successor in place of his elder son and heir Uslak.

Jebei and Subodai turned towards the Caucasus; having conquered the plains and faced the sea, they would now scale the mountains. They broke the Georgian chivalry, their first conflict with Christian Europeans, and then marched over the difficult and beautiful pass of Darial, beneath the shadow of snowy Kazbek, into the Russian plains between the Terek and the Don. At the river Kalka, near the sea of Azov, they beat the Russian princes and probably made the first contact between the Mongols and the Italian and Armenian merchants who thronged the busy ports of the Black Sea, for here were the great termini of European trade.

When they had turned from the Caspian to the Caucasus the subjects of the Sultan in Khwarizm itself heaved sighs of relief. Jelal came to Urganj to claim his kingdom and found to his satisfaction that an army of 90,000 men was already assembled. He had reckoned without his brother and his grandmother, however. The latter hated him cordially, while Uslak, a feeble creature, listened readily to all suggestions that Jelal had basely deprived him of his just inheritance. A military conspiracy drove Jelal out into the desert with a handful of seventy companions, glad to be away with his life, and the desperate fugitives made for Ghazna in Afghanistan, his own fief, fighting their way through the Mongol patrols that everywhere beset the country. With them went the last hope of any resistance to the invaders in the Khwarizm itself. Turkan-Khatun was an implacable enemy and an able old woman, but she was not a soldier and incapable of rallying the army, torn with jealousies. Moreover, at the critical moment she also proved a coward, and a cruel coward into the bargain. When the news came that Juchi and Jagatai were advancing on Urganj, she fled, first giving orders that the Seljukid hostage princes be massacred.

Turkan-Khatun was guided in her flight by a certain Omar-Khan, whom she murdered as soon as she reached safety in the fortress of Ilal. It was significant that none of the citizens of Urganj chose to follow her, but prepared to remain with their goods and defend them against the invader of their prosperous country.

Flight did not help the old woman. The Mongol whirlwind overtook her, her male grandchildren were slain or made captive, and she herself sent away to the bleak Mongolian steppe to drag out the rest of her wretched years in the tents of the victors, despised and forgotten.

Her subjects made a braver show. Though the army of the three princes laid siege to Urganj with the customary Mongol energy, cutting down the mulberry-trees to provide ammunition for their catapults, since there were no stones in that region, diverting the course of the Amu to deprive the besieged of water and using their favourite siege weapon the flaming oil, they met with such a stout resistance that no impression had been made at the end of seven months.

During the long siege the princes Juchi and Jagatai fell to quarrelling and discipline declined, with the result that the losses of the besiegers mounted rapidly. The news came to Chingis, now campaigning in Khorasan, on the frontiers of modern Afghanistan, and he sent a messenger post-haste appointing Ogödei to the supreme command. Unity restored, the city was taken by storm at last, though every quarter had to be fought for separately, every house carried singly by assault, before the brave resistance ended.

Chingis and Tuli had meanwhile moved into Afghan-Khorasan, reducing its fortresses one by one. The resistance they met with here was far stouter than any so far encountered and complicated, moreover, by the fact that Jelal ed-Din, having reached his fief of Ghazna in safety, was raising a field army. Shigi-Kutaku, the trusted and wise administrator of the *yasak*, was detached to deal with Jelal while the main force attacked the great cities. It was in Khorasan that Chingis won his reputation for destruction and wanton slaughter. Merv, with its splendid libraries, one of them with 12,000 volumes, its elaborate system of dykes and embankments maintained by 10,000 workmen, was utterly devastated and the great works on the River Mughrab broken down. Even in the fourteenth century the Arab geographer Ibn Batutah reports it to be only a great ruin in a desert swamp. Balkh was another famous and prosperous city which was still a ruin when seen by Ibn Batutah.

How many people perished in these massacres it is impossible to say. Nine million corpses are said to have been found in the ruins of Merv. Though this is no doubt an exaggeration, the fate of another city, Barmiyan, is a sign of what the Mongols were capable of when their destructive fury was once roused. In the siege of this city, the boy Mutukin, son of Jagatai, was killed by a well-aimed arrow. Chingis ordered that no living thing, neither man, nor beast, nor bird should be left and that the city itself should be razed and the ground levelled with the dust. The order was strictly carried out; Barmiyan became an uninhabitated waste, to which the conquerors gave the name 'Mav Balik,' 'the accursed city.' High up on the mountain-side above this desolate spot there remained unharmed yet another sign of man's work, a great cave of Buddhas. A Red and a Grey Buddha carved of rock guarded the entrance to a chamber supported on columns, while within were the grave, unsmiling statues of the man who sought for immortality in self-annihilation. On the walls were carved the likenesses of 'every species of bird that Allah had created.' Below was the stench of death and two or three gibbering, insane ghosts clinging to the level place that had been a city. The Mongol troopers rode on.

Shigi-Kutuku, meanwhile, had met with a heavy defeat at the hands of Jelal ed-Din, now master of a considerable army. At Perwana he completely overthrew the Mongols, whose timid leadership, hesitating before a night attack, had allowed his superior forces to concentrate. Many prisoners were taken and put to death by torture, Nesawi telling us that as Jelal watched their agonies 'his face was shining with joy.' If it were so, he paid dearly for the pleasure. It was the fate of Chingis at each stage of his career to rouse up one stubborn and implacable enemy. Jelal was the last of these, the most brilliant and the least worthy. This prince who had the title of Sultan of Islam, without the reality of a Sultan's power, was a true Turkish adventurer, though by a curious irony he became leader of the Iranian national resistance to the Mongols.

Chingis received the news of the defeat at Perwana calmly. 'Kutuku is accustomed to be always the victor, to vanquish and overcome, and has never yet tasted the cruelty of fortune. Now that he has felt that cruelty he will grow cautious, experienced and careful in all things.' He was summing up his own experience. Few men had known more of the cruelty of fortune than he or learned more of the need for caution and moderation at the right time and in the right place. When the army marched back over the battlefield some time later he made the defeated generals how him the exact disposition of the opposing armies and pointed out to them the mistakes they had made in choice of position.

The last fortress holding up their advance having fallen, in the autumn of 1221 the united Mongol army advanced into Afghanistan to crush Jelal ed-Din. The Sultan had been unable to keep his unruly leaders from falling out over the division of the spoil at Perwana and was forced to retreat towards the Indus with depleted forces. On the banks of this greater river Chingis overtook him and the last pitched battle of the Western war was fought.

The Mongol Army had marched with its usual rapidity, but when scouts brought Chingis the news that Jelal was encamped by the Indus and collecting boats for a crossing at dawn, he ordered a forced march through the night and surrounded the Sultan's position. When the sun rose the Turko-Afghan Army saw the Mongols all round them, curved like a stretched bow, the river forming the string. They were 'between fire and water.'

The Mongols attacked on both wings, aiming to roll the enemy up on the centre and cut them off from the river. Jelal, commanding the centre, fought bravely from dawn till noon, and then, seeing all hope lost, commanded that his mother, wives and children be flung into the current to drown, rather than that they should fall to his enemy, and he himself sword in one hand, black banner in the other, mounted on a fresh horse, cut his way through to the bank, leaped in and swam his horse across. Chingis sent a cavalry division after him, the first Mongol force to enter India, but the raid was not pressed home and Jelal found a safe refuge in the Punjab.

The defeat and flight of the Sultan meant that there was no force left to resist the Mongols anywhere in Iran or Turan. Prince Tuli completed the conquest of Khorasan, sacking Herat and Nishapur, while in Irak and the other provinces of the empire, when it was known the Khwarizm-Shah was dead and his son a fugitive, anarchy reigned everywhere, each lord trying to grab for himself the revenue of as many villages as possible, while the old racial hatred between Turks and Iranians flared up at every point. In Irak another son of Mohammed, Ghiyats ed-Din, made some show of rule, but it was a feeble one which must yield to the first challenger. Since the Mongols for the moment pressed no further westward, that challenger in the end turned out to be his brother Jelal ed-Din.

This hardy adventurer was recruiting himself in India, making profitable marriages, swaggering from place to place, drawing the fragments of his own beaten following to his side again. Few things are more remarkable than the attachment which his biographer, Nesawi, formed for him. This lord of Nesa was his very antipodes, a mild, cautious, bookish, pious man with something of an avaricious love for money as well as for learning. Jelal loved show, intrigue, great marriages, women and merrymaking, having a proper Turkish love for the bottle. While Chingis retired to Mongolia and his last campaign in China, Jelal gathered a small force again in the Punjab, whence a coalition of the Indian princes soon expelled the turbulent adventurer to seek a new refuge in his own dominions.

He marched his army over the desert to Irak, losing all his horses and many men in the terrible crossing, 4,000 exhausted men on oxen and asses getting through at last. Ghiyats at once prepared to resist him, but Jelal sent a message to placate him by describing his distress. 'The earth is too narrow for me, despite its vastness. I have lost all the goods that I possess, and I am come here to seek rest for a few days. But you have nothing to offer your guests but the honey of blades and shining sabres for your invited friends.' The envoys who brought this pathetic message bribed the emirs at Ghiyats' court and on a misty night in which only the gleam of lance-tips shone, 3,000 men refreshed and remounted attacked his camp under Jelal's leadership. So the Sultan became a ruler once more, and the greedy Turkish nobles pillaged the peasants of Irak to their heart's content.

Not till after Chingis's death was Irak conquered by the Mongols and Jelal driven into flight again. He fled, like his father, from fort to fort, from mountain fastness to mountain fastness, the relentless Mongol troopers ever at his heels, the pious Nesawi with his books always by his side. The end came one dark night in Kurdistan.

Nesawi was sitting writing in his tent, Jelal, overcome by his misfortunes, was sleeping drunkenly in his own tent when the sudden clash of arms and the cries of the sentinels roused them. Jelal ed-Din fled alone into the mountains and was cut down like a dog by a Kurdish chief whose hospitality he sought. With him ended in 1231 the last resistance to Mongol rule in the old empire. No one regretted him, save perhaps the faithful lord of Nesa; to the exhausted peasantry the order and discipline of the new masters could have been only a relief, for it is always the lesser evil to be robbed according to law than to be at the mercy of the rapacious whims of any violent adventurer who can establish his brief power.

3. The Sage and the Conqueror

THE conqueror was growing old. The terror he had unloosed in Khorasan was pricking a little at his conscience. For he could not forget, amid these great cities, among these cultured peoples, that he himself was only an illiterate barbarian and his soldiers as uncouth as himself. Life must end, however great the will to carry on the conflict further, and though one should conquer the greatest countries of the world, something must always remain unsubdued. He did not want to die. The further his armies marched, the more conscious he became that these ordered forces were accomplishing something, changing something in the world through which they hacked their way. To his mind it seemed as though his *yasak*, his code of laws, his Mongol instinct for discipline, was the highest achievement. If it were imposed on all nations, if order reigned in every country, if the post horses and caravans went safely over the roads, if the nomad dwellers in felt tents kept peace among themselves and were enriched by the tribute and profits of peace, then the name of Chingis-Khan and the glory of his *yasak* must live for ever.

At Herat a very holy Imam among the prisoners was brought before him, for he liked the company of men of sense and learning. To him he put the question which tormented him, half-justifying himself for the ruined cities, half-explaining himself.

‘The Khwarizm-Shah was not a monarch,’ he told the Imam, ‘he was a robber. Had he been a monarch he would not have slain my envoys and traders who came to Otrra, for kings should not slay ambassadors.’

The Imam agreed with him, for the Church had no love for Mohammed ben-Takish. But Chingis was not satisfied with this much of agreement. He must know whether he was justified in all things. ‘Will not a mighty name remain behind me? he asked. The Imam was a man of courage and for all his fear of the Khan’s anger he was brave enough to answer him justly, having first extracted a promise of safety.

'A name continues to endure only where there are people,' the Imam said. The memory of the sack of Herat was too fresh in his mind to let him lie on that point and the courtier's answer would not come from his lips. Chingis turned away in a great rage, flinging his bow and quiver to the ground, seized by an intense emotion, for the answer had pierced beneath his armour, told him what he was afraid to tell himself. Controlling himself by a great effort he answered the reproach. 'There are many kings in the world, and, wherever the hoofs of the horses of Mohammed have reached, there I will carry slaughter and cause devastation. The remaining people who are in other parts of the world, and the sovereigns of the other kingdoms that are, they will relate my history.'

That word he fulfilled only too truly. Nesawi tells how from the mountain fortresses it was possible to look down into the once fertile plains and watch the advance of the Mongols marked by a great cloud of dust among the pillaged and deserted village. The cloud rose from the multitude of wretched captives and the herds of plundered stock they drove from place to place. The captives were used for siege work, after the young women and children and the artisans had been separated to be sent back to Mongolia. They did not always plunder and destroy, these hungry horsemen. Every one of the Moslem historians tells the same story, where the fortresses were willing to buy peace with a ransom of cloth, materials, woollen garments and other commodities, they could have peace.

In the Khan's own court his advisers were continually advising him to moderate his terror, not without success. Yeliu Ch'uts'ai was above all persistent in this. The wise statesman knew well enough that the Empire could not endure on a foundation of smoking ruins. After the battle of the Indus, when the Khan was thinking of returning to his own steppes, he took the opportunity to dissuade him from the difficult march into India and over the Himalayas and through Tibet, at the same time cleverly insisting on the need for a more moderate policy towards the conquered peoples.

The Mongol scouts are said to have met a fabulous creature in the mountains, an animal like a stag with a horse's tail, a green body and one horn, able to imitate the human voice, which cried to the Emperor's guards: 'Let your master go back as quick as possible.' Ch'uts'ai, consulted on the meaning of the apparition, answered: 'This wonderful animal is called Kistuan; he understands the tongues of all countries in the world. He loves living beings and is horrified by bloodshed. His apparition is a warning to your majesty. You, Prince, are the eldest son of Heaven, but the peoples are also your children, and they expect from you sentiments inspired by heaven for their well-being.'

It was perhaps not political motives alone, but also this persistent urge to understand the meaning of his own life, arising perhaps from the feeling of approaching death and the passionate desire to continue nevertheless to live, which caused Chingis to send an invitation to the Chinese hermit Ch'ang Ch'un to come to visit him in his camp. Ch'ang Ch'un, already a very old man, for he was born in 1148, received the invitation at his mountain retreat in Shantung in 1221. He was a Taoist, devoting his life, according to his philosophy, to the investigation of the Tao, the secret spirit or source of life, to the problem of immortality. Taoism in its cruder forms was much concerned with alchemy and the philosopher's stone, but the investigations of Ch'ang Ch'un and his school were purely philosophical and spiritual.

There is little doubt that Chingis, when he first heard of the great teacher, considered him to be a magician with the secret of eternal life and that he wished to have this secret brought to him, as other precious things were brought to him for his possession from all parts of the empire. On his side, no doubt, the considerations which moved this weak old man to attempt the long journey across Asia to the conqueror's camp by the Indus, were somewhat more material than spiritual.

The hopes, the aspirations, the ideal life of man have always found form in the lofty and beautiful abstractions of religion and philosophy. Through them he has always sought an explanation of life and of the world. But religions, while appearing more than human, are the product of man's life, of the clashes of class and nation, and behind their other-worldliness are always lurking the sufferings and conflicts of this world. They are the idealized pictures, while the reality of man's history, which is but the continuation and development of the history of nature, from time to time tears through them in the search for new faiths in its infinitely complex battle to subdue the world of nature.

So it cannot be concealed that in a world of blood and turmoil such as was China in the thirteenth century there were probably other excellent reasons for retiring to a remote and beautiful mountain cave than the mere desire for contemplation. By this means the leader of a religious sect of great political influence and considerable property, and this Ch'ang Ch'un was, can withdraw himself from the anarchy of a collapsing State and wait for a propitious moment to show itself when it will be possible to intervene effectively on behalf of his own followers. To retire from the world when the conflicts of life have become momentarily too difficult is a useful possibility which Mr Gandhi is far from being the first to have exploited.

The courts of the Kin, the northern emperors, and of the Sung, the southern emperors, frequently urged the influential Ch'ang Ch'un to give them the light of his countenance, and he as steadfastly kept it averted. The support of his followers was of political importance to them, while for him it was more important to maintain neutrality till a strong ruler capable of affording the fullest protection should appear on the scene. Out of the barbarian steppe such a ruler had appeared and the wise old teacher in the mountain cave was well aware of it.

The letter of invitation which he received from the Khan, written, of course, with the help of the Chinese men of learning in his camp, and no doubt under the guidance of Yeliu Ch'uts'ai, is of the greatest interest, not only because it is the only document of the Emperor which we possess, but because it throws much light on his mood and outlook at this time, when the height of his temporal power coincided with the consciousness of age and physical weakness.

'Heaven,' Chingis wrote to Ch'ang Ch'un, 'has abandoned China owing to its haughtiness and extravagant luxury. But I, living in the northern wilderness, have no inordinate passions. I hate luxury and exercise moderation. I have only one coat and one food. I eat the same food and am dressed in the same tatters as my humble herdsmen. I consider the people my children, and take an interest in talented men as though they were my brothers. We always agree in our principles, and we are always united by mutual affection. At military exercises I am always in the front, and in time of battle never behind. In the space of seven years I have succeeded in accomplishing a great work and uniting the whole world in one empire. I have not myself distinguished qualities. But the government of the Kin is inconstant, and therefore Heaven assists me to obtain the throne (of the Kin). The Sung to the south, the Hui-ho to the north, the Hsia to the east and the barbarians in the west, all together have acknowledged my supremacy. It seems to me that since the remote time of our Shan Yu (Hun Khans), such a vast empire has not been seen. But as my calling is high, the obligations incumbent upon me are also heavy; and I fear that in my ruling there may be something wanting. To cross a river we make boats and rudders. Likewise we invite sage men and choose out assistants for keeping the empire in good order. Since the time I came to the throne I have always taken to heart the ruling of my people; but I could not find worthy men to occupy the places of the *three* and the *nine*. With respect to the circumstances I inquired, and heard that thou, master, hast penetrated the truth, and that thou walkest in the path of right. Deeply learned and much experienced, thou hast much explored the laws. Thy sanctity is become manifest. Thou hast conserved the rigorous rules of the ancient sages. Thou art endowed with the eminent talents of celebrated men. For a long time thou hast lived in the caravans of the rocks, and hast retired from the world; but to thee the people who have acquired sanctity repair, like clouds on the path of the immortals, in innumerable multitudes. I knew that after the war thou hadst continued to live in Shantung, at the same place, and I was always thinking of thee. I know the stories of the returning from the river Wei in the same cart, and of the invitations in the reed hut three times repeated. But what shall I do? We are separated by mountains and plains of great extent, and I cannot meet thee. I can only descend from the throne and stand by thy side. I have fasted and washed. I have ordered my adjutant, Liu Chung-lu, to prepare an escort and a cart for thee. Do not be afraid of the thousand li. I implore thee to move thy sainted steps. Do not think of the extent of the sandy desert. Commiserate the people in the present situation of affairs, or have pity upon me, and communicate to me the means of preserving life. I shall serve thee myself. I hope that at least thou wilt leave me a trifle of thy wisdom. Say only one word to me and I shall be happy. In this letter I have briefly expressed my thoughts and hope that thou wilt understand them. I hope also that thou, having penetrated the principles of the *great tao*, sympathisest with all that is right, and wilt not resist the wishes of the people."

The letter was written in the spring of 1219, in the beginning of the compaign against the Khwarizm-Shah. By the time it was received the Kin had been utterly defeated by Mukuli, the Khan's viceroy, and were also being attacked in the rear by the Sung. But

Mukuli was soon to die and a Sung victory meant that the Mongols would be face to face with this powerful southern empire, ruled by a native Chinese dynasty. In such circumstances the open support of the Taoist priests, the representatives, much more than the Confucians, of Chinese national religion, was an advantage of the greatest political importance. Buddhist support alone was not enough, for many looked upon the Buddhists as traitors to their country, since Buddhism was also the faith of so many of the barbarian invaders. Behind the simplicity and apparent humility of this letter of invitation was a deep political move. Not wisdom and immortality alone did Chingis seek, however much their quest harassed his mind in these late years, but a sound fabric for the great empire he was creating. Indeed, the closing sentences of this remarkable letter hint a double purpose in the invitation, when Chingis tells Ch'ang Ch'un he hopes 'thou wilt understand.'

The master's answer is no less diplomatically framed in its opening sentences. 'Kin Ch'u Ki, from Si hia hien, devoted to the *tao*, received lately from afar the most high decree. I must observe that all the people near the seashore are without talent. I confess that in wordly matters I am dull, and have not succeeded in investigating the *tao*, although I tried hard in every possible way. I have grown old and am not yet dead. My repute has spread over all kingdoms; but as to sanctity, I am not better than ordinary people, and when I look inwards I am deeply ashamed of myself. Who knows my hidden thoughts? Before this I have had several invitations from the southern capital (of the Kin) and from the Sung, and have not gone. But now, at the first call of the *Dragon court* (the Mongol court), I am ready. Why? I have heard that the Emperor has been gifted by Heaven with such valour and wisdom as has never been seen in ancient times or in our own days. Majestic splendour is accompanied by justice. The Chinese people as well as the barbarians have acknowledged the Emperor's supremacy. At first I was undecided whether I would hide myself in mountains or flee to an island in the sea, but I dared not oppose the order. I decided to brave frost and snow in order to be once presented to the Emperor.'

The answer, of which the above is the beginning, was dated April of 1220, the month of the swoop upon Bokhara and Samarkand. The journey itself, after many delays, began in the following year and the disciple who kept the diary of their voyage writes of the master that 'he was always cheerful, liked conversation and wrote verses.' The first part of the way was somewhat embarrassed by the fact that the holy men had to travel with a lively convoy of girls destined for the Khan's harem, an amusing comment on that puritan simplicity which Chingis so commended in himself in his letter. Ch'ang Ch'un was offended and addressed a protest to the commander of their escort. 'I am a mere mountain savage, but I do not think you ought to expect me to travel with harem girls.' The scandal was averted and they continued their way in seemlier fashion, looking back with regret upon the green plains of their country as they topped the high pass onto the brown and bleak Mongolian Plateau.

They travelled over the Mongolian steppe, carefully noting the customs of their conquerors, into the more settled country of the Naiman, where they found the land being cultivated and in one place a military settlement built, entirely inhabited by prisoners of war, 300 families from Honan weaving woollen cloth and 300 from Central Asia weaving gold brocade. The Chinese artisans and workmen left their looms to crowd out of the town to meet the master.

'They were all ravished; met him with exclamations of joy, bowed before him, and accompanied him with variegated umbrellas and fragrant flowers. There were also two concubines of the Kin Emperor, Ch'ang-Tsung, and the mother of a Chinese princess, who met the master with exclamations and tears. The latter said: "For a long time I have heard of your reputation and your virtues and was always grieved at not having seen you; but now, unexpectedly, I have met you in this country."'

'This country,' for them, was something like exile to the Outer Hebrides would mean to three cultured ladies of London society. To workmen and princesses alike this parched and feeble old man seemed to carry with him the spirit of the country they had lost.

The long and difficult crossing over the mountains, with all its hardships, followed, then the journey through the Uighur country, once the domain of the T'ang emperors, with the snowy peaks of the Tien Shan always in sight. Rain, snow and tempest accompanied them. One night, as they lodged in a vineyard, a great storm broke, shaking a huge tree outside the yard. The old teacher was tired and unwilling, only sustained by the desire to establish his sect before he died in the eyes of this new barbarian conqueror. As the wind blew he indulged in his only consolation, the making of verses.

'You speak of a voyage of ten thousand li;
Already we are come where winter knows no chill.
Whether I live or die, what matters it now?
Like thistle-down, I will go where I am blown.'

At last they reached Samarkand, only to find that Chingis was marching in pursuit of Jelal ed-Din across the Afghan mountains. But the master was given splendid quarters in a palace, with a fair view of the mountains, and here he was able to rest his old body for a few months. The city, half devastated, still preserved its loveliness and he had to confess that even Chinese gardens could not be compared with those of Sarmarkand. But he found the gardens very still and no singing of birds was to be heard there. The neighbourhood was infested with bands of robbers 'owing to the difficulty of finding subsistence' and every night in spring from the terrace of his palace he saw the sky red with fires. The country was in the throes of a peasant uprising. For there was no food anywhere. The war had put an end to cultivation and the town itself was gradually filling with starving peasants. The master fed the hungry country-folk with the surplus of his own provisions and prepared gruel for them, but the number who took advantage of this charity was always greater than the supply.

One other feature he noted. The city was invaded by Kara-Khitans, Chinese and Tanguts. 'Chinese workmen are living everywhere.' The cause of this was the appointment of a Kara-Khitan, a non-Mussulman, as Governor.

At last he reached the Imperial camp by the Indus, to be cordially greeted by the Khan. 'Sainted man, you have come from a great distance. Have you a medicine of immortality?' was the first question of the eager Chingis, after courtesies had been exchanged. 'There are means for preserving life, but no medicine for immortality,' the sage answered. He explained carefully to the Khan the way of life, what man must do and abstain from doing in order to live long. No doubt, though the conversation has not been preserved, the precepts were largely moral, in accordance with Taoist idealism. In a forest hut not so many days march from where that conversation took place, a wise man, a professor of bio-chemistry, resting, like the author of this book, from the weariness of overwork, explained one night how it is within the power of every man to preserve his life to the age of 130.

'No man now dies a natural death,' he said, 'it is possible to live to a great age, preserving all one's faculties, and then to die gently and painlessly simply because the organism one day ceases to work. So it happens even among the mountaineers of the Caucasus, where great ages are common. Disease in general can be abolished, just as diseases in particular have been abolished. The only causes which today prevent us from making man a gift of his life are social, and these will go with the building of a new world.' And all those who listened to the joyous words of the scientist, mostly young men and women pouring themselves out in the creation of that world, were strengthened and refreshed.

The Khan appointed another day for hearing the full doctrine of the Tao, but was prevented owing to the rising of the hillmen of Afghanistan. After that began the long march back to Mongolia, in accordance with the pre-arranged plan. Twice there took place long and earnest conversations between the conqueror and the sage, in which the latter gently exposed the superstitions of the Mongols, trying to draw them to a more civilized way of life. Once while hunting Chingis fell heavily from his horse, to be met with a mild reproof from Ch'ang Ch'un that it was time for a man of his years to take a greater care of himself and avoid such risks. For two months Chingis, who was born in the saddle and brought up to the hunt, followed his advice. At length they parted, the old teacher turning his face towards his quiet mountain refuge above the sea, away from this soldier's camp, in his pocket the Khan's decree freeing all Taoist priests and institutions from the payment of tax. He could now die peacefully, his mission accomplished.

4. The Journey Home

THE journey home began in the spring of 1223. He was sixty-eight and had already accomplished more than any man of his race, more, as he had justly claimed in the letter to Ch'ang Ch'un, than the Khans of the ancient Huns. The fall from his horse had been a warning and he might well have looked forward to spending the little time that was left to him in the peace of the native steppe he loved so much. Yet, as he had told the Chinese sage, the Mongols from childhood were born to the saddle and the use of the bow, and, he might have added, he himself was born under the star of war and hatred. He must die in the saddle, he must die at war, and before he died he must know further sorrow from his children.

At the first half beyond the Syr a great hunt was organized by Juchi, his eldest son, the doubtful child of Bortei. Juchi had shown signs of discontent already at the siege of Urganj and afterwards had gone to his own domain in the Kipchak steppe, refusing to come to his father's camp. The other brothers did not conceal their dislike of him. Even before the Western campaign they had expressed their feeling openly to their father, when the question of the succession was discussed.

'Father, surely thou dost not intend that Juchi should be thy heir, to rule over us, he who has come to us from the Merkit clan?' asked Jagatai. The reference was to the Merkit raiders who had raped their mother Bortei when she was the bride of the young Temujin. The two young men had then fallen violently upon one another in the presence of their father and mother, and noticeably, it was not Chingis, watching in gloomy silence, but Jagatai's tutor who separated them, reproving the youth and defending Bortei. 'When thou wert still unborn, Jagatai, and the world was full of disorders, when men robbed and slew one another and it was not possible to live in peace, thy wise and glorious mother was unhappily stolen. Do not such words as thine wrench thy mother's heart? Thy father, in creating the empire, has shared his labours with thy mother. They brought up you children, in the hope you would become men. Thy mother is bright as the sun, deep as the sea. How canst thou speak thus of one who has such gifts?'

Juchi seems to have been a good, if uninspired soldier, to have cared little for the new luxuries of the Mongol court, but to have spent his time on the wide steppes of modern Kazakstan, enjoying to the full his passion for the hunt. He looked towards the broad plains and forests of Russia, dreamed of building a great independent steppe nation, and the last years of his life were spent in intrigue against his father.

In slow stages the army, joined now by all the princes save Juchi, moved back to the land between the Tula and Selenga, near the city of Kara-Korum. Here they rested again through autumn and winter, arranging feasts and sports when the early summer had come, when the *kumys* was plentiful and the steppe for a brief period yielded in abundance all things which they needed. The *Nadom*, the national sports, was a great occasion. Here the two lines of stripped and brawny wrestlers made their obeisance to their old Khan, seated outside his great tent, under the nine-tailed banner. Encouraged by their seconds they gripped and threw and tried their strength before his red-rimmed, watching eyes, that never missed a thing.

They were veterans scarred from a hundred pitched battles, or youths come in for the first time to prove their fitness for the ranks of this world-conquering army. The victors of the first fights were awarded with drinks of *kumys*, with pieces of biscuit. Then as the contests approached the finals the prizes grew more valuable. The champion in those days might be sure of rich silks, of camels, or a fine-stepping stallion, perhaps even a painted captive from the harems of China or the Khwarizm-Shah. Then followed the shooting from the bow, and finally the horse-racing, for all classes from the two-year olds to the beautiful and much-prized pacers. The jockeys were gaily dressed boys of ten and twelve. The horse which won the gruelling test of a thirty-mile race might be sure of great honour and glory among the nomads. For these Mongols had rightly a religious veneration for their horses, who literally gave them everything, food and drink, the very means of life. The bleached horse's skull within the tent, the head and skin stretched weirdly on a pole in some desert place, are signs of this cult which you may still see in their country.

After the sports, the council, the *kuriltai*. This summer meeting was once the occasion when the elders of the tribe and clan met to discuss the organization of the annual march in search of pasture, the division of the grasslands among the families, the routes to be followed, and the other questions of their nomad way of life. Now it was a council of feudal lords and military commanders, come to discuss the orders of their ruler. In that summer of 1226 they had to listen to the order to prepare once more for war, this time against the Tangut King who was now in open revolt.

Chingis determined to subdue them for ever and to continue the war into China, where the Kin, since Mukuli's death, were again raising their heads. This time he would strike from a different direction, using the Tangut kingdom as a base against China. His mind worked as clearly as ever, with the same wide vision and grasp of the essential, but his body was already failing. As the army moved off in the autumn to take up their positions for the campaign, the sandy-red horse which he was riding took fright at a wild horse and threw him heavily.

That night he lay in a fever and his wife Yesui, who had accompanied him to war, called the generals into council. They advised the postponement of the attack, but the old Khan, when their decision was brought to him, refused to listen. 'I will get better here, in the field. They shall not think I am afraid of them, these Tangut.' An ambassador was sent ahead to demand the enemy's submission, which was summarily refused. 'Though I die,' Chingis declared, 'I will call them to answer, I swear it by the Eternal Heaven!'

Rashid tells us that throughout the campaign his mind was full of this awareness of his approaching death. One night he dreamed it was near and at dawn sent for his two sons, Ogödei and Tuli, ordering all other from his presence whilst he spoke with them.

'Children,' he greeted them, 'despite all expectation, the time of my last campaign and of my passing is near.' Then he ordered them to live in peace together in the great empire he had built for them, each in his own appointed *ulus*, or domain, and Ogödei, the wisest must be his heir. 'I wish to die at home,' he added. Before the end came he was given the news that Juchi was in revolt in far Kipchak. He ordered a force to march against this rebellious son, who was not his son, but before it was gathered the news arrived that Juchi was dead.

He could not have felt any joy at the news. But a man who has made such wars and dealt with men as Chingis did, must quickly have lost the feeling of personal happiness, his mind for ever full of the affairs of half the world. No doubt the shrewd old realist felt a little relief, mingled with his bitterness, for the death of this rebel meant that it would be easier for his remaining sons to live at peace with one another and preserve the Mongol Empire. For that there was only one means, to observe the *yasak* and enforce its observance on others.

The Tanguts were defeated, their king beleaguered in his capital, their young men captive and their maidens in the beds of the conquerors. The army turned toward China. Day by day, says Rashid, the illness of the Khan grew worse and he knew the end was not far. 'Let not my end disarm you,' he told his generals, 'and on no account weep or keen for me, lest the enemy be warned of my death.' The Tangut King and all his followers were to be be massacred when the capital fell, was his last command. In August 1227, on the Upper Wei River, near the junction of the frontiers of the modern provinces of Kan Su and Shen Su, he died.

He had not died at home, as he desired, but as he had lived, in the field, among his army. They raised his coffin, placed it on a two-wheeled wagon, and marched back with it to the hills and forests where he was born, by those rivers whose waters, says Ch'ang Ch'un, are deliciously clear and cold, and tinkle with a sound like jade bells.

As the host marched, they slaughtered every living thing they encountered, man or beast, lest any word of their loss go out to the enemy. As they marched, wrote Sanan Setsen, Kiluken Bagatur of the Sumid tribe lifted up his voice and sang:

'Whilom thou didst swoop like a falcon: a rumbling wagon now trundles thee off:
O my king!
Hast thou in truth then forsaken thy wife and thy children and the Diet of thy people?
O my king!
Circling in pride like an eagle whilom thou didst lead us
O my king!
But now thou hast stumbled and fallen, like an unbroken colt,
O my king!'

The place of his burial is a secret to this day. Probably it was on that hill of Burkan-Kaldum,[1] where once his life was saved from his enemies, the memory of which has always remained sacred to his people. Once, says Rashid, whilst hunting there, he saw a tree whose solitary beauty caught his attention. For an hour he sat beneath it in reverie feeling an inner exaltation. When he rose he said to his followers: 'This place is fit for my last rest. Let it be noted.'

[1] The word Burkan in Mongol conveys the idea of 'holy', 'divine.' No doubt the mountain on which the conqueror rests derived its name from the ancient Mongol worship of the spirits of mountain, river and forest.

5. The Heritage of Chingis-Khan

THERE are many signs that in these last years of his life Chingis was contemplating a change in his policy. His was far from being a purely destructive genius, as his organization of the Mongol nation had proved. and, since the conquest of China, he had had wise and moderate counsellors continually about him. Perhaps the conversations with Ch'ang Ch'un had also had their effect. The Chinese history is quite explicit about this new feeling in his mind and reports him as saying to his generals before his death: 'My time has come. Last winter when the Five Planets appeared together in one quarter was it not to warn me that an end should be put to slaughter, and I neglected to take notice of the admonition? Now let it be proclaimed abroad, wherever our banners wave, that it is my earnest desire that henceforth the lives of our enemies shall not be unnecessarily sacrificed.'

The influence of Yeliu Ch'uts'ai was undoubtedly strongly exercised towards moderation and constructive work. The Mongol army in its last compaign was attacked by a violent epidemic. The generals, according to their custom, had thought only of acquiring gold and precious stuffs. But the wise minister had acquired only books and natural products, including rhubarb, with which he dosed the sick soldiers. His already great influence was still further strengthened by this sign of his superior qualities.

His biography gives a vivid picture of the state of the conquered countries before Chingis's death. The Khan had passed his life in camp and at war. unable to pay proper attention to civil administration, to appoint magistrates and judges. Life and death, we are told, depended on the caprices of the powerful. The atrocities of the Governor of Yanking drove the minister to protest to the Emperor who henceforth agreed that power should only be exercised by those who had received an imperial patent. This in itself was a reform of the greatest importance, for it meant an end to the feudal anarchy ruling over the greater part of Asia, where the strongest and most unscruplulous seized the government at will.

In Khwarizm, for example, the local governors, even at the height of Mohammed's power, oppressed and plundered unhindered, and in one case the exactions were so appalling that Nesawi tells us the Sultan gave the inhabitants permission to burn the wazir alive. They do not appear to have succeeded, for he afterwards became Jelal's chancellor and was able to continue his plundering on the scale of a kingdom in place of a province.

Such a relation between the ruler and his officials became quite impossible in the ordered Mongol Empire. After the Khan's decree, says a Chinese author, 'the wind of slaughter began to cease.' It was not, however, an easy thing to win the old conqueror over to the new policy of mildness, for he was surrounded by generals as merciless as himself, but without any of his genius and vision. China, on the return of the army from the West, was a desert. Famine was everywhere, barns and warehouses were empty. To the simple and ruthless mind of the Mongol militarist the easiest way to deal with the economic problem left by the war was by a wholesale massacre of the population.

The generals seriously suggested to the Emperor that the Chinese were quite useless for the service of the State and that the population of the conquered provinces should be exterminated, the cities levelled and the land given over to pasture. Yeliu Ch'uts'ai objected cunningly to this appalling proposal. He pointed out to Chingis that as his armies penetrated the south of China they would need an infinity of things that it would be easy to obtain if he were ready to assess on an equitable basis the territorial contributions and commercial taxes, the salt tax, the taxes on iron, wine, vinegar and the produce of mountain and lake.

In this way he could get annually 500,000 ounces of silver, 80,000 pieces of cloth, over 40,000 quintels of grain, in short everything he needed to maintain his troops. 'How can it be argued', he concluded, 'that such a population is of no use for the service of the State?' As the Chinese biographer comments, 'philosophy might have provided more eloquent arguments against the proposed massacre, but none more likely to appeal to the Mongols who were quite capable of committing this crime.' Indeed, cupidity, combined with shrewd common sense, was characteristic of this strange conquest of half the world by a small, unknown nation. The policy of Ch'uts'ai prevailed because it was so obviously advantageous, and from now on the strength of the militarists in the Council declined. After the death of Chingis, the Khitan minister was appointed to draw up an administrative code for his son Ogödei and his influence became the predominant one.

How is one to sum up the career of such an extraordinary genius as Chingis-Khan? History offers no parallel to this twenty years of world conquest by an illiterate nomad who for the best part of his life could not even have had any conception of the world he was to conquer. Even at his death, for all his wide-ranging activity, he had never seen the sea. His contemporaries in both Europe and Asia had little doubt as to his greatness. 'Chingis was a man of vast ability, and led his armies like a god. . . . Such powers are wonderful and their loss is deeply to be regretted,' wrote the Chinese official history. Juzjani, expressing the favourable Moslem view in his history, was rather broader in his outlook. His estimate is interesting because it also contains the clearest physical description we have of the conqueror.

'Trustworthy persons have related that the Chingis-Khan, at the time when he came into Kharasan, was sixty-five years old, a man of tall stature, of vigorous build, robust in body, the hair on his face scanty and turned white, with cat's eyes, possessed of great energy, discernment, genius and understanding, awe-striking, a butcher, just, resolute, an overthrower of enemies, intrepid, sanguinary and cruel. . . . He was an adept in magic and deception, and some of the devils were his friends.'

Other Moslem historians, not compelled by any reason of servility towards rulers of Mongol descent, have taken a different view. For Ibn el-Athir the invasion of the West by this infidel army was a horrible catastrophe for Islam, a thing to be remembered with disgust and loathing. 'For some years,' he begins this part of his history, 'I was opposed to writing on the event, considering it horrible and feeling disgust at the telling of it. I started and stopped.' This, however, is the minority view, though it finds its reflection in certain modern European authors.

The gentle Joinville, the companion of St. Louis, wrote favourably of him. For Marco Polo, the representative of the youthful merchant class of Europe, 'He was a man of great worth, and of great ability (eloquence), and valour.' Even Chaucer writes of 'Cambynskan, which in his time was of so great renown, That ther was nowher in no regiown So excellent a lord in alle thing.'

History, on the whole, has never succeeded in finding for him a final place. Seeing exclusively the political achievements of the Mongol Empire, historians have viewed his work as something impermanent and transient, corresponding to what they consider to be the accidental nature of his conquests and whole career. Yet even from this limited viewpoint, and viewed on a world scale, the achievement is no mean one. The extent of the Mongol Empire, when it had been completed by his children and grandchildren, actually covered one half of the whole number of the human race at that time.

Certainly in time, and not a very long time, its unity became a formal one, between the Chinese, Central Asian, Russian and Persian kingdoms the relations were of the flimsiest and eventually the great empire split into its component parts, though still under Mongol rulers. Baber, a descendant of the great Khan, but Turkish speaking and completely Islamized, later conquered India and founded the great Moghul dynasty. No country in Asia remained without some influence in its life and institutions from the Mongol conquest.

Professor Barthold has given very clearly the *political* reasons for the break-up of the empire. 'The idea of the unity of the empire combined with several rulers arises from clan property. The clan and its property are a single whole. One person alone could rule over it in the event of his authority being recognized by all (as was that of Chingis). It could also be ruled by a conference of several representatives of the clan or their plenipotentiaries, as with Ogödei, his successor. This person or conference appointed rulers over the civilized districts which were the chief source of income of the dynasty. Although they drew their authority from the higher power, these rulers had to take into account the local non-Mongol princes. As the unity of the clan declined, the power of the local prince grew, often getting control of the armed forces.' Quite rightly Barthold points to Juchi's rebellion as the first sign of the inner weakening of the unity of the clan even in the lifetime of Chingis.

Though we will not go as far as Messieurs Grousset and Cahun, or Mr. Owen Lattimore, and see this great political achievement as the double result of a great national movement with the conscious aim of 'uniting all the peoples who dwell in felt tents,' to which Mr. Lattimore adds an economic basis by seeing the

Mongol pastoral economy as superior to the agriculture of their neighbours, nor yet to the mystical heights of the nationalism of the modern Mongol author Khara-Davan, who sees Chingis as a conscious world conqueror with a Mongol 'mission,' it must be granted that the Mongol nation, first organized as such and given national consciousness by Chingis, gave proof of remarkable qualities. The feeblest of his descendants had a virility lacking in the monarchs they displaced, while the military genius of this little people has never been equalled in history. Subodai was as great a general as his Khan, and even the royal princes proved themselves no mean warriors.

In the course of this book we have tried to explain each stage of the career of this nomad genius (this is the word which still comes most readily, as it came to his contemporaries and immediate successors when they discussed him). His unification of the Mongol tribes was no accident, but an inevitable stage in the course of the development of feudalism among this pastoral and warlike people. The relations between the nomad peoples and the great Asiatic civilizations were also not the result of accident, nor of temperament, but of the necessities of economic life. Had China been a strong and united country, with a stable economy, no Chingis-Khan would ever have conquered it, however 'godlike' his military skill. The same thing applies to Central Asia and Iran. If these two great societies, the Chinese on the one hand and the Turko-Iranian on the other, had not been in complete decay, Temujin would have stayed Temujin, with no conception of the world outside his native steppes.

It was the complete breakdown of production, the economic chaos and political anarchy of the neighbouring great powers, on whom the Mongols were in turn economically dependent, which forced Chingis to become a world conqueror. There was no question, as Marco Polo would have us believe, of his 'beginning to think of conquering a great part of the world.' It was the skilful opportunism of those Moslem and Uighur merchants who passed through his dominions with their caravans, who dwelt in Kara-Korum and the steppe towns near the Great Wall, that saw in his genius an agent for bringing order into the chaos of the great trade routes. These men, many of them as unlettered as Chingis, knew Asia like the palm of their hand. They were skilled in affairs and intrigue. They were able to give him an idea of the world which would otherwise have been quite unattainable to him. It is no wonder that in his instructions to his officers Chingis speaks so respectfully of these merchants. 'Just as our merchants, carrying brocaded garments and good things in the hope of profit, become exceedingly skilled in these goods and materials, so must the army leaders teach the young lads to shoot and ride, making them as bold and brave as the merchants are skilled in their arts.'

Probably only a great mind like that of Chingis could have so quickly grasped the picture of the world as they unfolded it to him. Certainly his youth as a hunted and hunting man, had taught him the feel of ground, that quick grasp of natural features and position so essential in war. Without any maps, by means of conversation alone, he saw the world as well as though it were spread before him on staff maps. This is essentially a military quality, one which his great generals, Jebei, Subodai, Mukuli, must also have possessed in equal measure. The difference between them and their leader lay in his ability to use this gift for great political ends also. Certainly we must also bear in mind that in his own person Chingis never came further west than Bokhara and that the advance of his armies into Persia and across the Caucasus partook more of the nature of a great raid than of actual conquest. Conquest was the work of his sons and grandsons, yet it was a work which they could never have accomplished but for the genius of this man from whom they sprang.

It is impossible to agree with the estimate of Vladimirtsov that 'on the whole the ambitious plans of Chingis-Khan met with failure. His empire dissolved, and the Mongols who had been led by the force of his military and political genius onto the theatre of world history did not maintain themselves long there. In the conquered lands they were absorbed by the more numerous or more civilized nations in whose midst they found themselves; at home they relapsed into the state out of which they had emerged under his leadership.' Each of these propositions is but a half-truth, which probably this great Mongolist would not himself have defended in his last years. If we accept it as a final estimate, then the bloody career of conquest remains but bloody conquest, the reality of Temujin-Chingis becomes the bogey of Genghis-Khan and the true monument to the Mongol people would be the famous pyramid of skulls in the painting of Verestchagin.

The pyramid of skulls cannot be ignored. These logical militarists waged war in its final abstraction, as a kind of pure art whose material was human life. Yes, the pyramid is a haunting background, but it is not the whole truth. The slaughter and devastation caused by the passage of the Mongol armies was appalling. A fugitive from Bokhara summed it up in the following verse: 'They came and thev sapped, they fired and they slew, trussed up their loot and were gone!' But violence is a weapon of history, and in the troubled history of Asia it has played a particular role. The devastations of these invaders destroyed much that was irreplacable, in some ways did irreparable harm, yet it cannot be admitted that the effect was pure negative.

First, we must remember that in both China and in Western Asia, human suffering and human rapaciousness had for centuries been the most prominent features of social life, as, with the break up of feudalism, they were also to become in Europe. Secondly, it is beyond doubt that the Mongol conquests, though they could not arrest a process which had already gone so deep into the social fabric, at least arrested the decay of Asiatic society for nearly two centuries. Though they did not and could not succeed in revitalizing that society they did ensure that the last of the Asiatic civilizations was no less glorious than those which had preceded it. The Yuan period in China, Moghul art and literature in India and Persia, these have given treasures to humanity which will for ever remain a precious possession.

After all, though we look at the results of the life-work of Chingis from even the narrowest viewpoint, it is impossible to ignore such a fact as that in Asia today, the only two countries to have preserved their complete independence and to have begun consciously to conquer the full fruits of that Western civilization which has brought such agony to the other Asiatic peoples who have not first won a like independence, are the People's Republic of Mongolia and the Turkish National Republic. The people of the first of these states are the direct descendants of Chingis, the people of the second have a great deal of Mongol blood and Mongol tradition mingled with their Turkish race.

All these things, however, are but the political reflections of the real work achieved by the Mongols. In effect, their conquests mark a great turning-point in human history, with results as striking for Europe and our own civilization, as for Asia. Had Chingis not turned in his last years towards the constructive side of his work, had he not given full play to the political genius which he had shown in his earlier years when uniting his own peoples, then the Mongols would in fact have left no more trace on history than the passage of a whirlwind. The wisdom of his decrees, the confidence he felt in his ministers and advisers and the ability he showed in choosing them, actually had the most revolutionary results upon the world in the years after his death. The Mongols proved in practice that they were as splendid organizers as they were soldiers.

The great post roads, functioning with clockwork efficiency, which united every part of the empire, the honesty and strict discipline of the military machine itself, the regard the Khans showed for the growth and encouragement of trade, the security they gave within their frontiers, wrought great changes in the relations between Asia and Europe. Above all the Mongol rulers proved to have an international outlook, to be enlightened and unprejudiced, more so than either the Moslem rulers of Asia Minor and Anatolia or than the Christians with whom they were soon in such friendly contact.

The rise of Chingis was almost contemporaneous with the rise of the Franciscan Order. Two generations after his death it was Franciscan and Dominican monks together with a few daring merchants who penetrated into the farthest recesses of his empire, bringing East and West into direct contact for the first time since Alexander the Great, making possible the triumph of the gospel of gold over that of poverty. The Christian powers saw in the Mongols allies against the Saracens. The growing commercial cities of the Mediterranean and Levant, now beginning to rejoice in the first flush of their young manhood, saw in them men who had re-opened trade routes which had been closed or disturbed for generations and who had no prejudice against the commercial ventures of foreigners within their dominions.

Nowhere in the world in the thirteenth century and early fourteenth century was there peace such as reigned within the Mongol Empire. 'The nomad peace,' Professor Beazley has aptly called it. Pegolotti, the Italian merchant we have quoted before, writes that 'the road you travel from Tana to Cathay is perfectly safe, and whether by day or night, according to what the merchants say who have used it. It is only dangerous during the *inter-regnum* when one lord has died and the next is not yet appointed.' The riskiest portion of the journey was at the beginning, from Tana on the Sea of Azov to Sarai on the Volga, but even here sixty men in the company means you go as safely as in your own house.

The Mongols, by restoring the unity of China, made possible a great increase in trade with the West. Not only were the overland routes now crowded, safe and well-organized, but a vast maritime trade developed with India. The lofty three-deckers, with their clouds of sail, their swarming passengers and luxurious cabins, dipped out of the Southern ports to the Straits, and thence to Calcutta. The Chinese master of an Indiaman became no less important a personage than his English counterpart in the eighteenth century. Ibn Batutah has described one of these lordly sea-captains landing and marching to his office, the centre of a whole ceremonial procession. Archers and negro-slaves went before him, armed with sword and spear, beating drums, blowing on horns and striking gongs. Marco Polo is full of descriptions of the wealth and size of the Chinese cities. No wonder Master Pegolotti was able to refer with enthusiasm to Peking as a great resort of merchants.'

The actual effect of the foundation of the Mongol Empire was that for something over a century the conditions for a real world market and world trade were created. China, Persia, India, Central Asia, the rich Black Sea region, Kipchak (Southern Russia and Kazakstan), Muscovy, all were drawn into this great commerce. The Italian merchants from Genoa and Venice, who held the monopoly of the Eastern trade, were in turn trading with France, Germany, Flanders and England. The house of Bardi in Florence, whose servant Pegolotti was, were 'King's merchants' to Edward III of England and failed in 1339 when that monarch defaulted on his debts.

In the end all the advantages of this rich trade came to Europe. Though the East was fabulously wealthy, its social system was rotten to the core and neither the Mongols nor any other rulers changed anything in that. China, beneath its covering of wealth and prosperity, remained under Kubilai the same land of suffering and want. His Uzbek minister of finance robbed the people as shamelessly as the ministers of the Kin and Sung had done. Usury grew and sapped the foundations of society like a dry rot, poisonous, destructive, unable to create anything new. Eastern feudalism showed only one great quality, the ability to prevent any progress, to hinder and restrain the growth of any new class capable of breaking down the rotten fabric and starting anew.

In Europe the enrichment brought to the towns by this Eastern trade found its way in the end to productive purposes, strengthened the new capitalist class and the sturdy independence of the city communes, spelled doom to feudalism and liberated the individual from the fetters of the Middle Ages. The sword of Chingis-Khan wrought a great revolution, but it was Asia in the end which lost by it, Europe which gained. The Mongol horseman, who spoke always in images of purest epic poetry, taken from the life of his steppe, master of the four fierce hounds who drank dew and rode on the wind, for all his close friendship with the Uighur and Uzbek merchants, could never have imagined that his life and conquests would have ended in the ventures of the cautious Master Francis Balducci Pegolotti, riding in his comfortable wagon, with his woman, his dragoman, his little convoy of merchandise.

Master Francis was the future. He did not think in images of epic poetry. A new song awoke in his heart, and he was literate enough to be able to write it down. This is how it went:

'Honesty is always best
And to look before ye leap:
Do whatever thou promisest;
And, hard though it may be, still keep
Fair chastity. Let reason tell
Cheap to buy and dear to sell,
But have a civil tongue as well.
Frequent the church's rites, and spare
To Him who sends thy gains a share.
So shalt thou prosper, standing by one price,
And shunning pest-like usury and dice.
Take aye good head to govern well thy pen,
And blunder not in black and white! Amen!'

Good master Francis! Here was the next conqueror of Asia riding over the steppe, gravely working out his profit and loss, a mild, pious and philistine hypocrite. No nomad horseman, watching from his shaggy red pony that quiet caravan amble by, could have imagined that it was to be the distant forerunner of conquerors more merciless than the four hounds of Temujin.

Miss Eileen Power has summed up this aspect of the Mongol Empire so well that it is best to quote her in full. 'Italian merchants chaffered and Italian friars said Mass in the ports and cities of

India and China, moved unhampered in their caravans on the great silk routes across Central Asia, or passed through Persia to take ship on the long sea road. The East and West for the first time came into direct contact from end to end. And if it be asked how this came about, the answer is an unexpected one—that it was the result of the conquests of a nomadic Mongol people from Central Asia of the same stock as the Turks, a people, moreover, which has come down in history with a reputation for unintelligent destruction equalled only by that of the Vandals. That people is best known under its medieval name of the Tatars. . . . They deserve to be judged as the power whose policy towards commercial intercourse between nations was so enlightened that they welcomed traders, lowered dues and protected caravans and roads throughout their dominions, maintaining free intercourse over the length and breadth of Asia, so that Professor Beazley can with justice call this period "the age of the nomad peace" and Sir Henry Howorth, speaking of this marvellous bringing together of the peoples of West and East can write: "I have no doubt myself . . . that the art of printing, the mariner's compass, firearms and a great many details of social life, were not discovered in Europe, but imported by means of Mongol influence from the furthest East." '

Temujin opened the wealth of Asia to the Western world and so made possible the birth of modern man. On the background of Eastern luxury, the Italy of cautious Pegolotti flowered into the Renaissance. The individual was born, stretched his fair and lusty limbs and found life good, glimpsed the evil grin of povery behind the beauty and the riches, and felt with a sudden pang the transience of life. Then Master Pegolotti gripped him and the fresh youth died. For he was born and lived in a tragic conflict with Time. He must fight the dead past, whose skeleton hands still clung to him, the dark medieval past, and he must face the future whose god of gold spelt death again.

'When I have seen such interchange of state,
Or state itself confounded to decay;
Ruin hath taught me thus to ruminate—
That Time will come and take my love away.
This thought is as a death, which cannot choose
But weep to have that which it fears to lose.'

Temujin marked the end of an age. Never again did an unknown nomad chief lead his fierce armies to the conquest of the world. Men of his race won great kingdoms and lost them, but they were men who had been absorbed and re-made by the culture of the conquered, petty landlords and princelings who began by seeking adventure and ended by founding a kingdom. Baber, Tamerlane, made great names in history, yet they never accomplished the half of what was done by Chingis-Khan and his splendid army. Their names are remembered and his is only a legend, as vague and unsubstantial as his own secret resting-place in the forest on the hill-side above the clear waters of his native rivers. It is a legend, however, which has kept ever fresh in the folk poetry of his own nation, and his name, with that of Alexander, is the one best known to the common people of Asia, which proves that they have a better judgmnt than many historias.

THE END

Bibliography

SOURCES

Ancient Mongol Narrative of Chingis-Khan. Translated by the Archimandrite Palladius. Works of the Members of the Russian Church Mission in Peking. Vol. IV, 2nd edition, Peking, 1910. (Sometimes referred to in the text as the "Secret History.")

Collection of Chronicles. The History of the Mongols by Rashid ed-Din. Translated by I. N. Berezine. Works of the Eastern Department of the Imperial Archaeological Society. 4 vols. St. Petersburg, 1868. [This is an extract from Rashid ed-Din's great encyclopaedic history of the world, the most remarkable of all medieval historical works.]

Tabakat-I-Nasiri by the Maulana, Minhaj ud-Din, Abu' Umar-I-'Usman. Translated by Major H. J. Raverty. London, 1881. 2 vols. *Bibliotheca Indica.* (Referred to in the text as Juzjani.)

Histoire du Sultan Djelal ed-Din Mankobirti by Mohammed En-Nesawi. Translated by O. Houdas. Paris, 1895.

Collection of Materials. Relating to the History of the Golden Horde. Baron Tizenhausen. Vol. I. St. Petersburg, 1884. Extract from Ibn el-Athir, "On the Invasion of the Mussulman countries by the Tatars."

Chrestomathie Arabe. Silvestre de Sacy. Tome II 2e édition. Paris, 1826. (For Maqrizi's account of the Mongol Yasak.)

Geschichte der Ost-Mongolen und ihres Furstenhauses, Verfasst von Ssanang Ssesten, Chungtaidschi der Ordus. Schmidt, I. J. St. Petersburg, 1829. [A not very reliable translation of the Mongol historian.]

Aboul Ghazi. Histoire des Mogols et des Tatares, trad. par le Baron Desmaisons. St. Petersburg, 1874.

Nouveaux Melanges Asiatiques. Abel-Remusat. Paris 1829. 2 vols. (For the biographies of Yeliu Ch'uts'ai, Tatatongu, etc.)

Medieval Researches from Eastern Asiatic Sources, by E. Bretschneider. London, 1888. 2 vols.

The Travels of an Alchemist (*Ch'ang Ch'un*), translated by Arthur Waley, London, 1931.

The Book of Ser Marco Polo, Yule and Cordier. 3 vols. London, 1903-20.

Cathay and the Way Thither. Yule. London, 1876. 4 vols. (For Pegolotti and much other invaluable material.)

The Life of Genghis-Khan by R. K. Douglas. London, 1877. This is a narrative woven together from the three official Chinese sources.

SECONDARY WORKS

ALFARIC, PROSPER. *Les Ecritures Manichéennes*. Paris 1918. 2 vols.

BARTHOLD, W. *Turkestan in the Epoch of the Mongol Invasion*. Second edition translated and revised by the author with the assistance of H. A. R. Gibb, London, 1928.

History of Turkestan. Tashkent, 1922.

History of Civilized Life in Turkestan. Leningrad, Academy of Science, 1927.

Article "Chingis-Khan" in the *Encyclopaedia of Islam*.

Article "Turks" in the *Encyclopaedia of Islam*.

BLOCHET, E. *Introduction à l'Histoire des Mongols de Fadl Allah Rashid ed-Din*. London, 1910.

CAHUN, LEON. *Introduction à l'Histoire de l'Asie*. Paris, 1896. Also the article on Chingis-Khan and the Mongol Empire in the *Histoire Générale of Lavisse et Rambaud*.

CORDIER, HENRI. *Histoire Générale de la Chine*, Paris, 1920. 4 vols.

D'OHSSON. *Histoire des Mongols depuis Tchingis-Khan jusqu'à Timour Bek on Tamerlan*. La Haye et Amsterdam, 1934-35, 2nd edition. 4 vols. This standard work is still of the greatest use owing to its scholarly collation of all the Mussulman historical sources.

GROUSSET, RENÉ. *Histoire de l'Asie*. Paris, 1921. 4 vols.

Histoire de l'Extreme Orient. Paris, 1929. 2 vols.

Les Civilizations de l'Orient. Paris, 1929-30. Vol. III. *La Chine*.

GRUMM-GRZHIMAILO, G. E. *Western Mongolia and the Territory of Urang-hai*. Leningrad, 1914-30. 4 vols.

HART, B. H. LIDDELL. *Great Captains Unveiled*. London, 1927.

The Decisive Wars of History. London, 1929.

HEYD, W. *Histoire du Commerce du Levant*. Leipzig, 1923. 2 vols.

HOWORTH, SIR H. *History of the Mongols*, Part I. London, 1876.

HUC, M. *Souvenirs d'un Voyage dans la Tartarie et le Thibet pendant les années* 1844, 1845, 1846. Paris, 1857. 2 vols.

KASAKEVICH, V. "Some Problems of Mongolian History in the light of Archaeology," the Journal *Contemporary Mongolia*. No. 4 (7), Ulan-Bator, 1934.

KHARA-DAVAN. *Chingis-Khan as Military Leader and his Heritage*. Belgrade, 1929 (In Russian).

KOZLOV, P. K. *Mongolia the Amdo and the Dead City of Kara-Khoto*. Moscow-Petrograd, 1923.

LAMB, H. *Genghis Khan, the Emperor of All Men*. London, 1928.

LATTIMORE, OWEN. *The Desert Road to Turkestan*. London, 1929.
High Tartary. London, 1930.
The Mongols of Manchuria. London, 1935.
Also articles in the *Geographical Journal*, December 1928 and December 1934.

LATOURETTE. *The Chinese*. London, 1934. 2 vols.

LESTRANGE, G. *The Lands of the Eastern Caliphate*. Cambridge, 1930.

LINDGRAN, E. J. "North-Western Manchuria and the Reindeer Tungus," *Geographical Journal*, June, 1930.

MASSÉ. *Essai sur le Poete Sa'adi*. Paris, 1919.

MAISKY, I. *Modern Mongolia*. Irkutsk, 1921.

MIHAILOV, G. "On the Problem of the Mongolian Movements of Conquest in the Thirteenth and Fourteenth Centuries, the Journal *Contemporary Mongolia*, No. 4 (7). Ulan-Bator, 1934.

PELLIOT, P. *Chretiens d' Asie Centrale et d'Extreme Orient*. T'Oung Pao, 1914.
Notes sur le "Turkestan" de M. W. Barthold. T'Oung Pao, 1930.

POWER, DR. EILEEN. "The Opening of the Land Routes in Cathay" (in "*Travel and Travellers of the Middle Ages*," edited by A. P. Newton). London, 1926.

ROSS, SIR E. P. *Aldred Lectures on Nomadic Movements in Asia*.
"Prester John and the Empire of Ethiopia" (in *Travel and Travellers of the Middle Ages*.) London, 1926.

SHASTINA, N. "Nadom" in *Contemporary Mongolia*, No. 3 (6). Ulan-Bator, 1934.

SIMUKOV, A. "Mongolian Migrations" in *Contemporary Mongolia*, No. 4 (7). Ulan-Bator, 1934.

STEIN, SIR AUREL. *On Ancient Central Asian Tracks*. London 1933.
The Sand-Buried Ruins of Ancient Khotan. 2 vols. London.

THOMSEN, V. *Les Inscriptions de l'Orkhon*. Helsingfors, 1903.

VLADIMIRTSOV, B. *Chingis-Khan*. Translated by D. Mirsky. London, 1930.

The Social Structure of the Mongols. Mongol Nomad Feudalism. Leningrad. Academy of Science, 1934.

VON LE COQ. *Buried Treasures of Chinese Turkestan*. London, 1928.

ZAHAROV, I. Articles and Papers in *Works of the Russian Church Mission in Peking*, Vol. I.

Index